Home-Tested
Dessert Recipes

Publications International, Ltd.
Favorite Brand Name Recipes at www.fbnr.com

Illustrations by Denise Hilton Campbell.

Photography on pages 5, 15, 27, 33, 51, 63, 77, 81, 101, 109, 127, 31, 137, 143, 153, 175, 189, 195, 201 and 217 by Proffitt Photography Ltd., Chicago.

Photography on pages 9, 21, 45, 91, 157, 171, 181 and 211 by Yuenkel Studios.

Pictured on the front cover: Apple-Pear Praline Pie *(page 38)*.
Pictured on the back cover *(clockwise from top left):* Vanilla Ice Cream Loaf *(page 126),* Blueberry Yogurt Cake *(page 8)* and Butterscotch Bundt Cake *(page 76).*

ISBN: 0-7853-8047-7

Library of Congress Control Number: 2003107319

Manufactured in China.

8 7 6 5 4 3 2 1

Microwave Cooking: Microwave ovens vary in wattage. Use the cooking times as guidelines and check for doneness before adding more time.

Table of Contents

Luscious Cakes   4

Perfect Pies   32

Creamy Cheesecakes   62

Cake Mix Secrets   76

Grandma's Favorites   94

No Bake Treats   126

Impressive Sweets   146

Kids' Goodies   174

Holiday Traditions   200

Index   218

Metric Chart   224

Many of the recipes in this book were submitted by home cooks as part of a contest previously sponsored by this publisher. Don't miss the prize-winning recipes on pages 38, 66, 72, 114, 146, 160 and 204.

Luscious Cakes

Lazy-Daisy Cake

Heidi Demeo ❧ Long Grove, IL

2 cups granulated sugar
4 eggs
2 teaspoons vanilla
2 cups all-purpose flour
2 teaspoon baking powder
1 cup warm milk
½ cup butter, softened and divided
1 cup coconut flakes
½ cup plus 2 tablespoons brown sugar
⅓ cup half-and-half

Preheat oven to 350°F. Grease 13×9-inch baking pan.

Beat granulated sugar, eggs, 2 tablespoons butter and vanilla in large bowl with electric mixer until fluffy. Sift flour and baking powder into medium bowl. Beat into egg mixture. Stir in milk. Pour into prepared pan. Bake 30 minutes or until toothpick inserted into center comes out clean.

Meanwhile, combine coconut, brown sugar, remaining 6 tablespoons butter and half-and-half in medium saucepan over medium heat. Cook until sugar dissolves and butter melts, stirring constantly.

Spread coconut mixture over warm cake. Place under broiler, 4 inches from heat source. Broil 2 to 3 minutes or until top turns light golden brown. (Do not burn.)   *Makes 12 to 14 servings*

Lazy-Daisy Cake

Banana Cake

Laura Fitzgerald ❧ New City, NY

2½ cups all-purpose flour
1 tablespoon baking soda
⅛ teaspoon salt
1 cup granulated sugar
¾ cup light brown sugar
½ cup unsalted butter
2 eggs
4 ripe bananas, mashed
⅔ cup buttermilk

Preheat oven to 350°F. Combine flour, baking soda and salt in large bowl. Set aside. Beat sugars and butter in medium bowl. Add eggs; beat well. Stir in bananas. Add flour mixture alternately with buttermilk to banana mixture. Pour batter into two 8-inch round cake pans. Bake 30 minutes or until toothpick inserted into centers comes out clean.   *Makes 2 (8-inch) round cakes*

Butterscotch Cake

Elizabeth Lewis ❧ Evarts, KY

1½ cups self-rising flour
1 cup sugar
1 cup sour cream
1 package (4-serving size) butterscotch-flavored instant pudding mix
½ cup water
½ cup oil
4 large eggs
1 package (12 ounces) butterscotch chips

Preheat oven to 325°F. Grease 10-inch Bundt pan. Set aside. Combine all ingredients except butterscotch chips in medium bowl. Fold in butterscotch chips. Pour into prepared pan.

Bake 45 to 60 minutes or until toothpick inserted near center comes out clean. Let cool completely. Remove from pan. Serve as desired.   *Makes 12 servings*

Devil's Food Cake

Sheryl Button ❧ *Cartersville, GA*

2 cups sugar
1 cup shortening
1 cup buttermilk
2 eggs
3 cups all-purpose flour
1 cup cocoa
1 package (4-serving size) chocolate-flavored instant pudding mix
1 cup hot water
½ cup oil
2 teaspoons vanilla
1 teaspoon salt
Powdered sugar, for garnish

1. Preheat oven to 375°F. Grease 10-inch Bundt pan. Set aside.

2. Beat sugar and shortening in large bowl with electric mixer. Add buttermilk and eggs; beat well.

3. Whisk together flour, cocoa and pudding mix in medium bowl. Add to sugar mixture, alternating with hot water and oil. Stir in vanilla and salt.

4. Pour batter into prepared pan. Bake 50 to 60 minutes. Cool in pan 30 minutes. Invert onto serving plate. Cool completely. Sprinkle with powdered sugar.   *Makes 12 servings*

Blueberry Yogurt Cake

Bonnie R. Barter ❧ Boothbay, ME

1 cup applesauce
½ cup granulated sugar
¼ cup butter
2 eggs
1 teaspoon vanilla
1½ cups cake flour
1 teaspoon baking powder
¼ teaspoon baking soda
½ cup plain or vanilla-flavored yogurt
1 cup fresh blueberries
1 cup chopped walnuts
½ cup brown sugar
1 teaspoon cinnamon

Preheat oven to 350°F. Line 8-inch square baking pan with foil and spray with nonstick cooking spray.

Beat applesauce, granulated sugar and butter in medium bowl with electric mixer at medium speed. Add eggs and vanilla. Sift in cake flour, baking powder and baking soda; stir to combine. Add yogurt; beat until smooth. Flour berries and gently fold in to cake mix.

Combine walnuts, brown sugar and cinnamon in small bowl. Sprinkle layer of walnut mixture over bottom of prepared pan. Pour batter over walnut layer. Sprinkle remaining topping over batter.

Bake 30 to 35 minutes or until toothpick inserted into center comes out clean. Cool completely. Garnish as desired.   *Makes 10 to 12 servings*

Coffee Cake

Frances Golding 🌿 Northbrook, IL

4 cups all-purpose flour
3 cups plus 1 tablespoon sugar
1 cup margarine
1 cup butter
1 cup cold milk
2 egg yolks
1 package yeast
1 teaspoon salt
3 egg whites
3 cups crushed pecans
1 tablespoon cinnamon
    Powdered sugar

1. Preheat oven to 350°F.

2. Combine flour, 1 tablespoon sugar, margarine, butter, milk, egg yolks, yeast and salt in large bowl. Mix until well combined. Form into ball and refrigerate 4 hours or overnight.

3. Beat egg whites in medium bowl. Gradually add remaining 3 cups sugar. Fold in pecans and cinnamon.

4. Roll out dough to 15×2-inch rectangle. Spread dough with egg white mixture. Roll up dough jelly-roll style. Place on baking sheet. Bake 40 minutes or until dough is lightly browned. Sprinkle with powdered sugar before serving. *Makes 10 to 12 servings*

Lemon-Lime Pound Cake

Lucia Antonino ❧ Tracy, CA

3 cups sugar
1½ cups margarine, softened
5 eggs
2 teaspoons lemon extract
3 cups cake flour
¾ cups lemon-lime flavored soft drink

1. Preheat oven to 325°F. Grease and flour 10-inch Bundt pan; set aside.

2. Beat sugar and margarine in large bowl with electric mixer at medium speed until light and fluffy. Beat in eggs, 1 at a time, beating well after each addition. Add lemon extract. Add flour and soft drink. Mix well.

3. Pour batter into prepared pan. Bake 1 hour or until toothpick inserted near center comes out clean. *Makes 12 servings*

Apple Cake Dessert

John Maruca ❧ Beaver Falls, PA

4 apples, peeled, cored and thinly sliced
1½ cups granulated sugar, divided
½ teaspoon cinnamon
2 cups all-purpose flour
¾ cup vegetable oil
3 eggs, beaten
1 tablespoon plus 2 teaspoons lemon juice
1½ teaspoons baking soda
1 teaspoon vanilla
Powdered sugar

Preheat oven to 325°F. Combine apples, ½ cup granulated sugar and cinnamon in medium bowl. Set aside. Combine flour, remaining 1 cup granulated sugar, oil, eggs, lemon juice, baking soda and vanilla in large bowl. Stir in apple mixture until well combined. Pour into 13×9-inch baking dish. Bake 35 to 40 minutes or until toothpick inserted into center comes out clean. Sprinkle with powdered sugar. *Makes 10 to 12 servings*

Easy Patriotic Layer Cake

Donna Abramchuk ❧ Porterville, CA

1 container (16 ounces) low-fat ricotta cheese
¼ cup applesauce
2 tablespoons sugar
⅛ teaspoon vanilla
2 containers (8 ounces each) blueberries, divided
2 containers (8 ounces each) fresh raspberries, divided
2 loaves (10 ounces each) prepared angel food cake *or* 2 loaves
   (12 ounces each) pound cake

1. Combine ricotta, applesauce, sugar and vanilla in medium bowl. Combine ¼ cup blueberries and ¼ cup raspberries in small bowl; set aside.

2. Cut each cake into 10 slices. Line bottom and sides of 9-inch loaf pan with 11 slices of cake (3 on bottom, 3 per side and 1 at each end). Spoon about ¼ of ricotta mixture into pan, spreading over cake in even layer. Top with ½ remaining blueberries and 3 slices cake. Spread cake with ¼ of ricotta mixture. Top with remaining raspberries and 3 slices cake.

3. Spread cake with ¼ of ricotta mixture and top with remaining blueberries and final 3 slices of cake. Top with remaining ¼ of ricotta mixture and sprinkle with reserved mixed berries. Cover and refrigerate at least 1 hour before serving. *Makes 12 servings*

Butterscotch Malt Zucchini Cake

K C Hill ❧ Siletz, OR

1¾ cups brown sugar
½ cup margarine or butter
½ cup oil
2 eggs
½ cup buttermilk
1 teaspoon vanilla
2½ cups all-purpose flour
4 tablespoons malted milk powder
1 teaspoon baking soda
½ teaspoon salt
½ teaspoon baking powder
½ teaspoon nutmeg
2 cups grated zucchini
½ cup nuts
½ cup butterscotch chips
½ cup white chocolate chips

Preheat oven to 350°F. Grease and flour 13×9-inch cake pan or 10-inch Bundt pan.

Beat brown sugar, margarine, oil and eggs in large bowl with electric mixer at medium speed. Add buttermilk and vanilla. Beat until well combined.

Combine flour, milk powder, baking soda, salt, baking powder and nutmeg in medium bowl. Stir into creamed mixture. Stir zucchini, nuts, butterscotch chips and white chocolate chips into batter.

Pour batter into prepared pan. Bake 40 to 45 minutes (60 to 65 minutes for Bundt pan) or until toothpick inserted into center comes out clean.

Makes 10 to 12 servings

Cookies 'n' Cream Cake

Cindy Colby ❧ Park Ridge, IL

1 package (about 18 ounces) white cake mix
1 package (4-serving size) instant white chocolate pudding and pie filling mix
4 egg whites
1 cup vegetable oil
½ cup milk
20 chocolate sandwich cookies, coarsely chopped
½ cup semisweet chocolate chips
1 teaspoon vegetable shortening
4 chocolate sandwich cookies, cut into quarters for garnish

Preheat oven to 350°F. Spray 10-inch fluted tube pan with nonstick cooking spray.

Beat cake mix, pudding mix, egg whites, oil and milk in large bowl with electric mixer at medium speed until ingredients are well blended. Stir in chopped cookies; pour into prepared pan.

Bake 50 to 60 minutes or until cake springs back when lightly touched. Cool 1 hour in pan on wire rack. Invert cake onto serving plate; cool completely.

Combine chocolate chips and shortening in glass measuring cup. Heat in microwave on HIGH (100%) power 1 minute; stir. Continue heating at 15 second intervals, stirring, until melted and smooth. Drizzle glaze over cake and garnish with quartered cookies.   *Makes 10 to 12 servings*

Helpful Hint

Crush sandwich cookies quickly and easily by placing them in a sealed plastic food storage bag, then running a rolling pin over the bag several times to pulverize them.

Carrie's Carrot Cake

Carrie Martell ❧ South Barre, VT

3 cups all-purpose flour
3 cups sugar
1 tablespoon baking soda
1 tablespoon cinnamon
1 teaspoon salt
1½ cups vegetable oil
4 eggs
1 tablespoon vanilla
1 can (20 ounces) crushed pineapple, well-drained
1½ cups chopped walnuts
1⅓ cups carrots, cooked, drained and grated
¾ cup shredded coconut
Cream Cheese Frosting (recipe follows)

1. Preheat oven to 350°F.

2. Grease three 9-inch round cake pans. Line bottoms with greased parchment paper. Set aside.

3. Combine flour, sugar, baking soda, cinnamon and salt in large bowl. Add oil, eggs and vanilla; beat well with electric mixer.

4. Fold in pineapple, walnuts, carrots and coconut.

5. Pour mixture into prepared pans and bake 30 to 35 minutes or until knife inserted into centers comes out clean.

6. Prepare Cream Cheese Frosting.

7. Place one cake layer on serving plate. Frost top of cake. Repeat layers using remaining cake layers and frosting. Frost top and sides of cake. Refrigerate until ready to serve.   *Makes 12 to 16 servings*

Cream Cheese Frosting

12 ounces cream cheese, softened
½ cup butter plus 1 tablespoon, softened
1½ teaspoons vanilla
4½ cups powdered sugar

1. Beat cream cheese and butter in large bowl with electric mixer until smooth; add vanilla.

2. Stir in powdered sugar one cup at a time, beating well after each addition.

Carrie says:

Cooking the carrots adds to the moisture of the cake.

Golden Creme Cake

Ellen Parish ❧ Boardman, OH

2 packages (10 cakes each) cream-filled golden snack cakes
2 containers (8 ounces each) frozen whipped topping, thawed
1 can (about 20 ounces) crushed pineapple, drained
3 bananas, peeled and cut in ¼-inch slices
1 package (4-serving size) vanilla-flavored instant pudding mix, prepared according to package directions
4 toffee candy bars (1½-ounces each), crushed and divided

1. Slice 10 snack cakes in half lengthwise and place, cut sides down, in single layer covering bottom of 13×9-inch baking dish. Top with one container whipped topping. Sprinkle with pineapple and banana slices; top with pudding. Sprinkle pudding with half of toffee pieces.

2. Slice remaining snack cakes in half lengthwise and place in single layer over toffee pieces. Spread with remaining whipped topping and sprinkle with remaining toffee pieces.

3. Refrigerate 1 hour before serving.　　　　　　　　*Makes 16 servings*

Chocolate-Peanut Butter Oatmeal Snacking Cake

Kelly Smarts ❧ *Sarasota, FL*

1 cup rolled oats
1¾ cup boiling water
1 cup brown sugar
1 cup granulated sugar
½ cup butter, softened
2 eggs, beaten
1 teaspoon vanilla
1¾ cups all-purpose flour
¼ cup cocoa
1 teaspoon baking soda
1 cup chocolate chips
1 package (12 ounces) chocolate and peanut butter chips

Preheat oven to 350°F. Grease 13×9-inch baking pan; set aside. Combine oats and boiling water in medium bowl; let stand 10 minutes. Stir until water is absorbed. Add brown sugar, granulated sugar and butter to oats. Beat with electric mixer until well combined. Add eggs and vanilla; beat well. Combine flour, cocoa and baking soda in medium bowl. Gradually add to oat mixture. Stir in 1 cup chocolate chips. Pour into prepared pan. Sprinkle chocolate and peanut butter chips over top. Bake 40 minutes.   *Makes 12 to 14 servings*

Helpful Hint

Rolled oats can be found as quick-cooking rolled oats and old-fashioned rolled oats. They are essentially the same; the quick-cooking oats simply cook faster because they have been rolled into thinner flakes. Do not use instant oatmeal in this recipe.

Applesauce Cake

Jamie H. Mozingo La Pine, OR

2 cups sugar
1½ cups applesauce
½ cup shortening
½ cup water
2 eggs
2¾ cups all-purpose flour
1½ teaspoons baking soda
¾ teaspoon cinnamon
½ teaspoon cloves
½ teaspoon allspice
¼ teaspoon baking powder
1 cup raisins
½ cup chopped walnuts

1. Preheat oven to 350°F. Grease 13×9-inch baking dish; set aside.

2. Combine sugar, applesauce, shortening, water and eggs in large bowl.

3. Combine flour, baking soda, cinnamon, cloves, allspice and baking powder in medium bowl. Gradually add dry ingredients to wet ingredients. Stir in raisins and walnuts.

4. Pour batter into prepared pan. Bake 25 to 30 minutes or until toothpick inserted into center comes out clean.   *Makes 12 to 15 servings*

Jo's Moist and Delicious Chocolate Cake

Jo Skinner ❧ Miami, FL

2 cups all-purpose flour
1 cup sugar
4 tablespoons cocoa
1½ teaspoons baking powder
1½ teaspoons baking soda
1 cup mayonnaise
1 cup hot coffee
2 teaspoons vanilla

1. Preheat oven to 350°F. Grease and flour 10-inch Bundt pan. Set aside.

2. Sift together dry ingredients. Stir in remaining ingredients until batter is smooth. Pour into prepared pan.

3. Bake 35 minutes or until toothpick inserted near center comes out clean. Cool; remove from pan.   *Makes 12 servings*

∾ Jo says: ∾

May be frosted with your favorite icing or glaze. This is also delicious sprinkled with powdered sugar!

Julia Young's Chocolate Cake

Mary Davis Dasso ❦ Austin, TX

2 cups all-purpose flour
2 cups sugar
1 teaspoon baking powder
1 cup water
½ cup margarine
½ cup oil
4 tablespoons cocoa *or* 3 squares (1 ounce each) semi-sweet baking chocolate
½ cup buttermilk
2 eggs
1 teaspoon baking soda
1 teaspoon cinnamon
1 teaspoon vanilla
Cocoa Icing (recipe follows)

1. Preheat oven to 375°F. Grease and flour 13×9-inch metal baking pan.

2. Combine flour, sugar and baking powder in large bowl. Set aside.

3. Combine water, margarine, oil and cocoa in medium saucepan. Bring to a boil. Remove from heat. Add buttermilk, eggs, baking soda, cinnamon and vanilla; mix well. Add flour mixture; mix well. Pour batter into prepared pan.

4. Bake 30 minutes or until toothpick inserted into center comes out clean.

5. Prepare Cocoa Icing.

6. Spread Cocoa Icing over hot baked cake. Serve immediately or store, covered, until ready to serve.   *Makes 12 to 15 servings*

Cocoa Icing

1½ cups powdered sugar
½ cup chopped pecans
¼ cup margarine
3 tablespoons milk
2 tablespoon cocoa
1 teaspoon vanilla

Combine all ingredients in medium saucepan. Bring to a boil. Keep warm.

Hawaiian Fruit Cake

Mel Elliot ❧ Morton, MS

2 cups all-purpose flour
2½ cups sugar, divided
1 can (15¼ ounces) crushed pineapple, undrained
1 can (5 ounces) evaporated milk
½ cup margarine
1 cup chopped pecans
1 cup shredded coconut

Preheat oven to 350°F. Combine flour, 1½ cups sugar and pineapple in medium bowl. Stir until well combined. Pour into 13×9-inch baking dish. Bake 30 to 35 minutes. Combine evaporated milk, remaining 1 cup sugar and margarine in small saucepan. Cook 2 minutes or until margarine is melted and sugar is dissolved. Stir in pecans and coconut. Spread over cake. Serve as desired.   *Makes 12 servings*

Coconut Crunch Delight
Mary Livengood ❧ Meyersdale, PA

1¼ cup flaked coconut
1 cup all-purpose flour
1 cup slivered almonds
½ cup margarine, melted
¼ cup packed brown sugar
1 package (4-serving size) vanilla-flavored instant pudding mix
1 package (4-serving size) toasted coconut-flavored instant pudding mix
2⅔ cups cold milk
2 cups whipped topping

Preheat oven to 350°F. Grease 13×9-inch baking pan. Set aside.

Combine coconut, flour, almonds, margarine and brown sugar in large bowl. Press coconut mixture into prepared pan. Bake 25 to 30 minutes or until golden brown, stirring every 10 minutes to form coarse crumbs; cool. Divide coconut mixture in half. Press half mixture back into same pan.

Combine pudding mixes and milk in medium bowl. Fold in whipped topping. Spoon pudding mixture over crumb mixture in pan. Top with remaining crumb mixture. Cover and refrigerate overnight.   *Makes 12 to 16 servings*

Helpful Hint

This dessert also tastes great when the toasted coconut-flavored instant pudding mix is substituted with chocolate-flavored instant pudding mix.

Lemon Cream Cheese Pound Cake

Tena Camille DeAcklen ❧ Chicago, IL

1⅔ cups cream cheese, softened
½ cup butter, softened
4½ teaspoons lemon extract
1 or 2 teaspoons yellow food coloring
5 eggs
5 packages (9 ounces each) single layer yellow cake mix
5 tablespoons flour
1¼ teaspoons baking powder
4½ cups cold water

1. Preheat oven to 350°F. Grease and flour 10-inch tube pan. Cover bottom of pan with parchment or waxed paper trimmed to fit; grease paper lining. Set aside.

2. Combine cream cheese, butter, lemon extract and food coloring in large bowl. Beat with electric mixer until light and fluffy. Beat in eggs, one at a time, scraping bowl after each addition. Add cake mixes, flour, baking powder and water; beat just until blended.

3. Bake 1 to 1½ hours or until toothpick inserted near center of cake is clean and dry when removed. Cake should be golden brown when done. Cool completely in pan. *Makes 16 servings*

❧ Tena says: ❧

This can also be used to make 3 (9-inch) loaf cakes. Reduce baking time to 35 to 40 minutes. You may also add raisins, chopped nuts or glacéed fruit dusted with flour to prevent sinking to bottom of cake. Freeze cake up to 6 weeks.

Orange Kiss Me Cakes

Rebecca Norman ❧ Fremont, OH

1 large orange
1 cup raisins
⅔ cup chopped walnuts, divided
2 cups all-purpose flour
1⅓ cups sugar, divided
1 teaspoon baking soda
1 teaspoon salt
1 cup milk, divided
½ cup shortening
2 eggs
1 teaspoon cinnamon

1. Preheat oven to 350°F. Grease and flour 6 (4-inch) miniature Bundt pans or 10-inch Bundt pan. Set aside.

2. Juice orange to equal ⅓ cup. Reserve juice. Chop remaining orange pulp and rind. Process pulp and rind, raisins and ⅓ cup walnuts using metal blade of food processor until ground (or put through fine blade of food grinder.)

3. Sift flour, 1 cup sugar, baking soda and salt together in large bowl. Add ¾ cup milk and shortening. Beat with electric mixer at medium speed until well blended. Beat 2 minutes more. Add eggs and remaining ¼ cup milk. Beat for 2 minutes. Fold orange mixture into flour mixture. Pour into prepared pans.

4. Bake 20 to 25 minutes (30 to 35 minutes for 10-inch Bundt pan) or until toothpick inserted near centers comes out clean.

5. Poke holes in cakes with wooden skewer. Pour reserved juice over cakes. Combine remaining ⅓ cup sugar, ⅓ cup walnuts and cinnamon in small bowl. Sprinkle over cakes. Garnish as desired. *Makes 12 servings*

Triple Chocolate Pudding Cake

Jackie Schweitzer ❧ Greenville, WI

1 cup biscuit baking mix
½ cup sugar
¼ cup cocoa powder
¾ cup milk, divided
⅓ cup butter
1 teaspoon vanilla
¾ cup hot fudge ice cream topping, divided
1 cup semisweet chocolate chips, divided
¾ cup hot water or coffee
    Whipped cream or frozen whipped topping (optional)

1. Preheat oven to 350°F. Grease 8×8-inch pan.

2. Combine baking mix, sugar and cocoa in medium bowl. Stir in ½ cup milk, butter, vanilla and ¼ cup fudge topping until well blended. Stir in ½ cup chocolate chips and pour batter into pan.

3. Combine remaining ¼ cup milk, ½ cup fudge topping and hot water. Stir until well combined; pour over batter in pan. Do not stir. Sprinkle remaining ½ cup chocolate chips over fudge topping mixture.

4. Bake 45 to 50 minutes or until center is set. Remove from oven and let stand 15 minutes. Spoon pudding cake into dessert dishes. Serve with whipped cream or frozen whipped topping, if desired.   *Makes 8 servings*

Yum-Yum Cake

Jackie Feinartz ❧ *Buffalo Grove, IL*

1¼ cups granulated sugar
½ cup butter
2 eggs
2 cups all-purpose flour
1 teaspoon baking soda
1 teaspoon baking powder
½ teaspoon salt
½ cup sour cream
½ cup milk
1 teaspoon vanilla
⅓ cup brown sugar
1 teaspoon cinnamon
½ to 1 cup chopped pecans

Preheat oven to 350°F. Grease 9×9-inch baking pan. Set aside.

Beat 1 cup granulated sugar and butter in large bowl with electric mixer until fluffy. Add eggs, one at a time, beating well after each addition.

Sift flour, baking soda, baking powder and salt into medium bowl. Add dry ingredients to butter mixture alternately with sour cream and milk, beginning and ending with flour. Stir in vanilla.

Combine remaining ¼ cup granulated sugar, brown sugar, cinnamon and pecans in medium bowl.

Pour half batter into prepared pan; cover with half cinnamon mixture and repeat layers.

Bake 40 minutes or until toothpick inserted into centers comes out clean.

Makes 10 to 12 servings

Banana Split Roll

Trudi Hina ❧ *Zanesville, OH*

3 eggs
1 cup sugar
2 medium bananas, peeled and mashed
1 teaspoon lemon juice
2 teaspoons cinnamon
1 teaspoon baking powder
½ teaspoon salt
1 cup bread flour
1 package (8 ounces) cream cheese
¼ cup butter
1 cup powdered sugar
⅓ cup crushed pineapple, well-drained
½ teaspoon vanilla
1 cup semi-sweet chocolate chips
1 tablespoon shortening
1 cup chopped nuts (optional)

1. Preheat oven to 375°F. Grease and flour jelly-roll pan; set aside.

2. Beat eggs in large bowl with electric mixer at high speed until pale and thick, about 3 to 4 minutes. Gradually beat in sugar. Beat in bananas and lemon juice. Add cinnamon, baking powder and salt; mix well. Add flour; mix just until combined. Pour into prepared pan and level with spatula.

3. Bake 15 minutes or until toothpick inserted near center is clean when removed. Immediately turn out of pan onto towel dusted with flour. Starting on short side, roll towel and cake together. Place on wire rack and cool completely.

4. Beat cream cheese, butter, powdered sugar, pineapple and vanilla in medium bowl with electric mixer until smooth. Unroll cake and spread evenly with cream cheese mixture; re-roll. Wrap tightly in plastic cling wrap and refrigerate for at least 30 minutes.

5. Melt chocolate chips and shortening in small saucepan over medium-low heat, stirring frequently. Drizzle thin ribbons of chocolate over cake. Immediately sprinkle with chopped nuts, if desired.   *Makes 8 servings*

Citrus Cake

Etta Delores Faultry 🍓 Alvin, TX

3 cups all-purpose flour
2¾ cups sugar
1 teaspoon baking powder
¼ teaspoon salt
1¼ cups butter, softened
5 eggs
⅔ cup milk
1 teaspoon lemon extract
1 teaspoon orange extract
Citrus Cream Cheese Frosting (recipe follows)

Preheat oven to 350°F. Grease and flour 10-inch Bundt pan. Combine flour, sugar, baking powder and salt in large bowl. Add butter, eggs and milk; mix well. Add extracts; mix well. Pour batter into prepared pan. Bake 50 to 60 minutes or until toothpick inserted near center comes out clean. Cool completely. Prepare Citrus Cream Cheese Frosting. Invert cake onto serving plate. Frost top and sides of cake. Refrigerate 1 to 2 hours.

Makes 12 servings

Citrus Cream Cheese Frosting

1 package (8 ounces) cream cheese, softened
1 container (8 ounces) frozen whipped topping, thawed
¼ cup sugar
1 teaspoon orange extract
1 teaspoon lemon extract

Combine all ingredients in medium bowl. Beat with electric mixer at medium speed until creamy.

Perfect Pies

Favorite Peanut Butter Pie

Carolyn Blakemore ❧ Fairmont, WV

1 prepared (9-inch) shortbread pie crust
¾ cup creamy peanut butter, divided
½ cup peanut butter chips, divided
1 package (3 ounces) cream cheese
1 cup powdered sugar
1 container (8 ounces) frozen nondairy whipped topping, thawed

1. Spread ¼ cup peanut butter over bottom of pie crust. Sprinkle with ¼ cup peanut butter chips.

2. Beat cream cheese and sugar in medium bowl with electric mixer; beat in remaining peanut butter until light and fluffy. Fold in whipped topping.

3. Pour into pie crust and sprinkle with remaining peanut butter chips. Serve immediately or refrigerate.   *Makes 8 servings*

Hawaiian Delight Pie

Dorothy J. Kapahua ❧ *Fort Myers, FL*

Pastry Crust

    1 cup all-purpose flour
    ½ cup finely chopped macadamia nuts
    ½ teaspoon salt
    ⅓ cup cold butter
    3 to 4 tablespoons water

Filling

    ⅓ cup granulated sugar
    1 tablespoon cornstarch
    1 can (10 ounces) crushed pineapple, undrained
    1 package (8 ounces) cream cheese, softened
    3 tablespoons orange-flavored powdered drink mix
    ½ teaspoon salt
    2 eggs, beaten
    ½ cup milk
    ½ cup finely chopped macadamia nuts
    1 teaspoon rum extract
    ½ teaspoon vanilla

1. Preheat oven to 350°F. Grease 8-inch pie plate.

2. For pastry crust, combine flour, nuts and salt in medium bowl. Cut in butter with pastry blender or two knives until coarse crumbs form. Sprinkle water, one tablespoon at a time, over flour mixture. Mix until flour is moistened and dough sticks together. Shape into ball. Chill about 15 minutes.

3. Roll out dough on floured surface 1½ inches larger than pie plate. Place dough in prepared plate and flute. Lightly prick bottom of crust. Set aside.

4. For filling, combine sugar and cornstarch in medium saucepan. Stir in pineapple and juice. Heat over medium heat, stirring constantly, until mixture thickens and is clear. Remove from heat; cool completely. Spread pineapple mixture on bottom of pie crust.

5. Combine cream cheese, drink mix and salt in medium bowl, mixing until thoroughly combined. Add eggs, one at a time, beating at medium speed with electric mixer. Add milk, nuts, extract and vanilla; mix by hand. Pour cream cheese mixture over pineapple mixture, spreading evenly.

6. Bake 35 to 45 minutes or until crust and pie filling are light golden brown and pie filling is set. Let cool and refrigerate until ready to serve.

Makes 8 servings

Pineapple Cream Cheese Pie
Myria Estes ✴ Cullman, AL

1 package (8 ounces) cream cheese, softened
1 can (20 ounces) crushed pineapple, drained with juice reserved
2 cups cold milk
2 packages (4-serving size) vanilla-flavored instant pudding mix
2 prepared (9-inch) graham cracker crusts
Whipped topping

1. Beat cream cheese, reserved pineapple juice and milk in medium bowl with electric mixer until well-combined. Add pudding mix; beat until smooth. Stir in pineapple.

2. Pour into prepared crusts and refrigerate until set. Top with whipped topping to serve.

Makes 16 servings

✴ Myria says: ✴

For reduced-sugar pies, use pineapple in its own juice and substitute sugar-free instant pudding mix.

Fancy Fudge Pie

Tina M. Cartee ❧ Mentor on the Lake, OH

1 cup chocolate wafer crumbs
⅓ cup butter, melted
½ cup butter, softened
¾ cup packed brown sugar
3 eggs
8 ounces semi-sweet chocolate chips, melted
1 cup pecans, chopped
½ cup flour
1 teaspoon vanilla
½ teaspoon instant espresso
  Whipped cream or vanilla ice cream (optional)
  Chocolate syrup (optional)

1. Preheat oven to 375°F. Combine cookie crumbs and melted butter in small bowl. Press onto bottom and up sides of 9-inch pie pan. Bake 6 minutes. Remove from oven and let cool.

2. Beat softened butter and brown sugar in large bowl with electric mixer until light and fluffy. Add eggs, one at a time, beating well after each addition. Stir in chocolate, pecans, flour, vanilla and espresso, scraping bottom and sides of bowl.

3. Pour mixture into prepared pie crust. Bake 30 to 40 minutes or until set. Cool and refrigerate. Serve chilled with whipped cream or ice cream and chocolate syrup, if desired.   *Makes 8 servings*

Penelope's Favorite Pumpkin Pie

Jo Skinner ✤ *Miami, FL*

2 tablespoons powdered egg

¼ cup pineapple juice

2 cups fresh pumpkin, mashed *or* 1 can (15 ounces) solid packed pumpkin

1 can (14 ounces) sweetened condensed milk

1 teaspoon cinnamon

1 teaspoon nutmeg

½ teaspoon ginger

⅛ teaspoon salt

1 prepared (9-inch) graham cracker pie crust

Whipped cream

1. Preheat oven to 350°F.

2. Beat powdered egg with pineapple juice in medium bowl with electric mixer until smooth.

3. Add pumpkin, milk and spices; beat until fluffy. Pour into pie crust.

4. Bake 50 to 60 minutes or until center is set. Cool and serve with whipped cream. *Makes 8 servings*

Apple-Pear Praline Pie

Stacy Dent ❧ Honolulu, HI

6 cups Granny Smith (or other variety) apples, peeled, cored and
  thinly sliced
3 cups pears, peeled, cored and thinly sliced
¾ cup granulated sugar
¼ cup plus 1 tablespoon all-purpose flour, divided
4 tablespoons cinnamon
¼ teaspoon salt
1 pie crust for 9-inch double crust pie
½ cup plus 2 tablespoons butter, divided
1 cup brown sugar
4 tablespoons half-and-half
1 cup chopped pecans

1. Preheat oven to 350°F.

2. Combine apples, pears, granulated sugar, ¼ cup flour, cinnamon and salt in large bowl; toss gently to combine and set aside for 15 minutes. Place bottom crust in 9-inch deep dish pie pan and dust lightly with remaining 1 tablespoon flour. Spoon apple and pear mixture into pie crust and dot with 2 tablespoons butter. Top with second pie crust and flute as desired, slitting crust to vent steam.

3. Bake 50 to 55 minutes. Remove pie from oven, leaving oven on.

4. Melt remaining ½ cup butter in small saucepan over low heat. Stir in brown sugar and half-and-half. Cook until mixture boils, stirring constantly. Remove from heat and stir in pecans. Spread over top of pie.

5. Place pie on cookie sheet and bake 5 minutes; remove from oven and cool 1 hour or more before serving. *Makes 8 servings*

Stacy Dent

 *Perfect Pies*

Easy Minty Lemon Pie
Paula Murphy ❧ Crystal Lake, IL

1¼ cups graham cracker crumbs
¼ cup butter, melted
1 tablespoon sugar
1 tablespoon cinnamon
1 can (14 ounces) low-fat sweetened condensed milk
½ cup lemon juice
4 teaspoon grated lemon peel, divided
1 tablespoon fresh mint leaves, chopped fine (plus 8 leaves for garnish)
1 pint whipping cream, whipped to soft peaks (optional)

1. Preheat oven to 350°F. Combine graham cracker crumbs, butter, sugar and cinnamon in medium bowl. Press firmly into bottom and up sides of 9-inch pie plate. Bake 7 to 10 minutes or until rich golden brown. Cool in refrigerator.

2. Combine all remaining ingredients, except 1 teaspoon lemon peel and whipping cream, in medium bowl and stir to combine. Gently fold in whipped cream. Pour into pie crust and garnish with remaining 1 teaspoon lemon peel and mint leaves. Refrigerate for at least 3 hours before serving. Top with whipped cream, if desired. *Makes 8 servings*

Creamy Vanilla Apple Pie

Heather Williams ❧ Paola, KS

1 egg
6 to 8 apples, peeled, cored and sliced 1/4-inch thick
1 cup vanilla-flavored yogurt
1 cup sugar
4 to 6 tablespoons all-purpose flour
1 teaspoon vanilla
1/2 teaspoon cinnamon
1 unbaked (9-inch) pie crust
  Spicy Crumb Topping (recipe follows)

1. Preheat oven to 350°F. Beat egg in medium bowl; add apples, yogurt, sugar, flour, vanilla and cinnamon; mix well. Stir to coat apples, then pour into pie crust.

2. Prepare Spicy Crumb Topping

3. Top apples with Spicy Crumb Topping. Bake 1 hour or until topping is toasted brown.   *Makes 8 servings*

Spicy Crumb Topping

1 cup all-purpose flour
1/2 cup sugar
1/2 cup brown sugar
1/2 cup (1 stick) butter, melted
1/4 teaspoon cinnamon

Combine all ingredients in medium bowl and stir to combine. Set aside until ready to use.

Spiced Raisin Custard Pie

Lorinda Platti ❧ Germantown, NY

1½ cups raisins
1 teaspoon sugar
1 teaspoon cinnamon
1 cup biscuit and baking mix
½ cup sugar
¼ cup butter or margarine, melted
3 eggs
1 can (14 ounces) regular or fat-free sweetened condensed milk
1 cup applesauce
2 teaspoons vanilla
2 teaspoons ground cinnamon
1 teaspoon ground nutmeg
1 container (8 ounces) frozen nondairy whipped topping, thawed

1. Preheat oven to 325°F. Spray 10-inch glass pie plate with nonstick cooking spray. Set aside.

2. Place raisins in small bowl, separating any that may be stuck together. Combine sugar and cinnamon in small bowl. Sprinkle half over raisins. Set remaining cinnamon-sugar mixture aside. Toss to coat.

3. Combine all remaining ingredients, except whipped topping and remaining cinnamon-sugar mixture, in large bowl. Beat with electric mixer until well combined, about 2 minutes, scraping sides of bowl frequently. Pour into prepared pie plate. Bake 10 minutes.

4. Remove from oven and top with spiced raisins; sprinkle with remaining cinnamon-sugar mixture. Return to oven and bake 35 to 40 minutes more (center will be soft). Cool to room temperature; refrigerate at least 2 hours. Serve chilled with whipped topping. Refrigerate leftover portions.

Makes 12 servings

Peanut Butter Pie

Shelia Meinhardt ❧ Burns Flat, OK

1¼ cups chocolate cookie crumbs (about 20 cookies crushed)
1¼ cups sugar, divided
¼ cup plus 1 tablespoon butter, divided
1 package (8 ounces) cream cheese, softened
1 cup creamy peanut butter
1 teaspoon vanilla
1 cup heavy whipping cream
Grated chocolate or additional cookie crumbs (optional)

1. Preheat oven to 375°F.

2. Combine cookie crumbs and ¼ cup sugar in medium bowl. Melt ¼ cup butter. Add to cookie crumb mixture, mix well. Press into 9-inch pie plate. Bake 10 minutes; cool.

3. Beat cream cheese, peanut butter, remaining 1 cup sugar, remaining tablespoon butter and vanilla in large bowl with electric mixer until smooth. Beat whipping cream in separate medium bowl with electric mixer until stiff peaks form. Fold into cream cheese mixture. Spoon into crust.

4. Refrigerate until ready to serve. Garnish with grated chocolate, if desired.

Makes 8 servings

Kathy's Key Lime Pie

Debbie Gerrie ❧ Grants, NM

1 package (8 ounces) cream cheese
1 package (4-serving size) lime-flavored gelatin
2 containers (8 ounces each) frozen whipped topping, thawed
1 prepared (9-inch) graham cracker pie crust

1. Beat cream cheese, lime gelatin and ⅔ of whipped topping in large bowl with electric mixer until smooth.

2. Pour into prepared pie crust and top with remaining whipped topping. Refrigerate until ready to serve or cut and serve immediately.

Makes 8 servings

Coconut Cream Pie

Cleo Swann ❧ Ducktown, TN

1 package (4-serving size) instant vanilla-flavored pudding mix
2¾ cups cold milk, divided
1 prepared (9-inch) graham cracker pie crust
1 envelope whipped topping mix
½ teaspoon vanilla
1 package (4 ounces) flaked coconut

1. Beat pudding mix and 1¾ cups milk in medium bowl with electric mixer until thick. Pour into pie crust and refrigerate 1 hour.

2. Beat whipped topping mix, vanilla and remaining 1 cup milk with electric mixer in large bowl. Beat 4 minutes at high or until thick and fluffy, spread on pie. Sprinkle coconut evenly over pie. Refrigerate until ready to serve.

Makes 8 servings

Italian Chocolate Pie alla Lucia

Bessie Turner ❧ *Royal Oak, MI*

4 tablespoons pine nuts
3 tablespoons brown sugar
1 tablespoon grated orange zest
1 unbaked (9-inch) pie crust
4 ounces bittersweet chocolate, coarsely chopped
3 tablespoons unsalted butter
1 can (5 ounces) evaporated milk
3 eggs
3 tablespoons hazelnut liqueur
1 teaspoon vanilla

1. Toast pine nuts in dry nonstick skillet over medium heat, stirring constantly until golden brown and aromatic. Remove from heat and finely chop; cool. Combine pine nuts, brown sugar and orange zest in small bowl. Sprinkle in bottom of prepared pie shell and gently press into place with fingertips or back of a spoon.

2. Preheat oven to 325°F. Melt chocolate and butter in small saucepan over low heat. Stir well to blend. Let cool to room temperature.

3. Combine chocolate mixture with evaporated milk in medium bowl with electric mixer at medium speed. Add eggs, one at a time, beating well after each addition. Stir in hazelnut liqueur and vanilla. Pour into pie shell over pine nuts.

4. Bake on middle rack of oven 30 to 40 minutes or until filling is set.

5. Remove from oven and cool. Refrigerate until ready to serve. Serve with whipped cream and chocolate curls, if desired. *Makes 8 servings*

❧ *Bessie says:* ❧

This pie is beautiful when garnished with chocolate curls. To make chocolate curls, melt ½ cup semi-sweet chocolate chips and 1 teaspoon vegetable oil in medium microwavable bowl on MEDIUM (50% power) 1 minute. Stir well. Spread chocolate mixture in 2-inch wide ribbon shapes on piece of parchment paper. Let set for 1 minute, then use the edge of a spatula to lift and scrape up firmed, but still warm, chocolate. The chocolate will curl into ribbons. Use these to garnish the pie.

Granny's No-Crust Chocolate Pie

Jean Friedrich ❧ Berea, OH

½ cup granulated sugar
3 tablespoons cocoa powder
3 tablespoons all-purpose flour
⅛ teaspoon salt
2 cups milk
2 eggs, separated
2 tablespoons butter
1 teaspoon vanilla
2 tablespoons superfine sugar

1. Preheat oven to 400°F.

2. Combine granulated sugar, cocoa, flour and salt in medium saucepan over low heat. Gradually whisk in milk and egg yolks. Cook, stirring constantly, until smooth and thick. Remove from heat and add butter and vanilla.

3. Pour into 9-inch buttered pie pan. Whip egg whites in medium bowl with electric mixer at high speed until foamy. Add superfine sugar and continue beating until stiff peaks form. Top pie with egg white mixture.

4. Bake 8 to 10 minutes or until pie is set and meringue is golden brown. Remove from oven and let cool 15 minutes before serving.

Makes 8 servings

Baked Alaska Apple Butter Pie

Eleanor Froehlich ❧ Rochester Hills, MI

1 unbaked (9-inch) pie crust
3 egg yolks, lightly beaten
2 cups apple butter
¼ cup light brown sugar
1 can (13 ounces) evaporated milk
1 pint butter pecan ice cream
   Brown Sugar Meringue (recipe follows)

1. Preheat oven to 425°F. Line ungreased 9-inch pie plate with pie crust and crimp edge as desired

2. Combine egg yolks, apple butter, brown sugar and evaporated milk in medium bowl. Mix until well blended. Pour into prepared pie crust. Bake 15 minutes. *Reduce oven temperature to 350°F.* Continue baking 45 minutes more or until thin knife inserted into center of pie comes out clean. Cool pie on wire rack about 1 hour. Cover and refrigerate at least 1 hour or until ready to serve.

3. Meanwhile, allow ice cream to soften slightly. Cover inside of 8-inch pie plate with plastic cling film. Place ice cream in pie plate and spread to evenly fill pie plate. Cover and place in freezer until solid.

4. Just before serving, preheat oven to 500°F. Prepare Brown Sugar Meringue. Using plastic film, unmold ice cream and invert onto prepared, chilled pie. Remove plastic film and cover ice cream and any exposed surface of pie with Brown Sugar Meringue. Bake until golden brown, 2 to 3 minutes. Serve immediately. *Makes 8 servings*

Brown Sugar Meringue

3 egg whites
¼ teaspoon cream of tartar
½ teaspoon vanilla
6 tablespoons brown sugar

Beat egg whites and cream of tartar with electric mixer until foamy. Beat in vanilla. Add brown sugar, one tablespoon at a time. Beat until stiff peaks form.

Mother's Coconut Pie

Mary G. Taylor ❧ Murfreesboro, TN

½ cup self-rising flour
1¼ cups sugar, divided
1¼ cups milk
3 eggs, separated
1 teaspoon vanilla
2 tablespoons butter or margarine
1¼ cups shredded coconut, divided
1 baked (9-inch) pie crust

1. Preheat oven to 350°F.

2. Combine flour and 1 cup sugar in 2-quart saucepan. Add milk, egg yolks, vanilla and butter, whisking well. Cook, stirring constantly, over medium heat until ingredients thicken. Remove from heat and add 1 cup coconut. Spoon into crust.

3. Beat egg whites in medium bowl with electric mixer until foamy. Slowly add remaining ¼ cup sugar and continue whipping until soft peaks form. Spoon on top of pie. Sprinkle remaining ¼ cup coconut on top; bake 10 to 15 minutes or until meringue is golden brown. Remove from oven and let cool.   *Makes 8 servings*

Raspberry Cream Pie
Linda Reiss ❧ Sarasota, FL

½ cup granulated sugar
¼ cup packed brown sugar
3 tablespoons all-purpose flour
1½ tablespoon cinnamon
1 pint heavy whipping cream
1 teaspoon vanilla
1 package (12 ounces) frozen raspberries
1 (9-inch) unbaked deep-dish pie shell

Preheat oven to 400°F. Combine sugars, flour and cinnamon in medium bowl. Add cream; stir until smooth. Add vanilla. Separate raspberries and place in pie crust. Pour cream mixture over raspberries. Bake 10 minutes. Reduce oven temperature to 375°F. Continue baking 55 to 65 minutes or until firm in center. Cool completely and refrigerate. *Makes 8 servings*

Egg Custard Pie
Carolyn Thorton ❧ Camden, SC

1 cup sugar
1 cup evaporated milk
2 eggs
1 teaspoon vanilla
1 (9-inch) unbaked pie shell
½ teaspoon margarine

Preheat oven to 325°F. Combine sugar, evaporated milk, eggs and vanilla in medium saucepan. Heat over high heat about 2 to 3 minutes, stirring constantly. Pour into pie shell. Dot with margarine. Bake 40 minutes or until knife inserted into center comes out clean. *Makes 8 servings*

Canadian Butter Tarts

Lillian Porter 🌿 *Deltona, IL*

¼ cup butter
½ cup firmly packed brown sugar
½ cup corn syrup
1 egg
½ cup chopped walnuts
¼ cup golden raisins
½ teaspoon vanilla
¼ teaspoon salt
8 medium unbaked tart shells

1. Preheat oven to 375°F. Beat butter in medium bowl until creamy. Gradually beat in sugar and corn syrup.

2. Add egg and beat until light; stir in walnuts, raisins, vanilla and salt.

3. Spoon into tart shells. Bake 8 minutes.

4. *Reduce oven temperature to 350°F.* Bake 12 to 13 minutes more or until filling is set and tart shells are lightly browned.   *Makes 8 servings*

Speedy Strawberry Pie

Ellis Rice 🌿 *Hillsboro, OR*

⅓ cup plus 2 tablespoons butter, softened and divided
1 cup vanilla wafer crumbs
3 containers (4 ounces each) strawberry yogurt
1 package (4-serving size) vanilla-flavored instant pudding mix
1 package (8 ounces) cream cheese, softened
1 cup strawberry preserves
1 teaspoon vanilla
1 cup fresh sliced strawberries

1. Preheat oven to 350°F. Melt ⅓ cup butter in small saucepan. Combine butter and wafer crumbs in small bowl. Press onto bottom and up sides of 9-inch pie dish. Bake 8 minutes. Remove from oven and cool.

2. Beat remaining 2 tablespoons butter, yogurt and pudding mix in medium bowl with electric mixer at medium speed until smooth. Add cream cheese, strawberry preserves and vanilla; beat well.

3. Pour into pie shell. Refrigerate until firm. Serve chilled with fresh sliced strawberries.   *Makes 8 servings*

Chocolate Root Beer Rocky Road Pie

Connie Emerson ❧ Reno, NV

1½ cups crushed chocolate wafers, plus additional for garnish
¼ to ½ cup powdered sugar
6 tablespoon butter, melted
1 can (14 ounces) sweetened condensed milk
3 egg yolks, beaten
1 tablespoon root beer extract
1 cup miniature marshmallows
¾ cup chopped pecans
Whipped cream, for garnish (optional)

Preheat oven to 325°F.

Combine wafer crumbs, powdered sugar and butter in large bowl. Blend thoroughly and press firmly into 9-inch pie plate.

Beat milk, egg yolks and extract in large bowl with electric mixer at medium speed 2 minutes. Stir in marshmallows and pecans. Pour mixture into crust. Bake 30 minutes or until knife inserted in center comes out clean. Cool completely on wire rack. Garnish with additional wafer crumbs and whipped cream, if desired.   *Makes 6 to 8 servings*

Citrus Custard Pie

Merrilee Powers ❧ *Troy, MI*

½ cup sugar
½ cup orange juice
1 package (4-serving size) vanilla-flavored instant pudding mix
3 tablespoons butter
2 tablespoons lemon juice
3 eggs
1 cup orange marmalade
1 teaspoon vanilla
1 prepared (9-inch) graham cracker pie crust
2 cups peeled sectioned orange slices

1. Preheat oven to 350°F.

2. Combine sugar, orange juice, pudding mix, butter and lemon juice in top of 2-quart double boiler over simmering water. Whisk until well blended. Beat eggs lightly in small bowl and stir into pudding mixture, whisking constantly. Cook until temperature reaches 160°F. Remove from heat and stir in marmalade and vanilla.

3. Pour into prepared pie shell. Let cool. Refrigerate until firm. Serve chilled with orange slices. *Makes 8 servings*

Brandy Alexander Pie

Leslee Crayne ❧ Appleton, WI

32 vanilla wafers
 3 cups vanilla ice cream, softened
 1 cup spiced egg nog
 1 package (4-serving size) vanilla-flavored instant pudding mix
 1 teaspoon vanilla
 ¼ teaspoon ground nutmeg
 2 ounces brandy
 1 cup frozen nondairy whipped topping, thawed
   Caramel ice cream topping (optional)

1. Line bottom and sides of greased 9-inch pie pan with vanilla wafers.

2. Beat remaining ingredients, except caramel topping, in large bowl with electric mixer at low speed until well blended. Do not overbeat.

3. Pour mixture into prepared pie pan. Freeze until firm. Serve with caramel topping, if desired. *Makes 8 servings*

❧ Leslee says: ❧

For a different, nutty flavor, substitute butter pecan ice cream for the vanilla ice cream.

Rustic Apple Tart with Crème Chantilly

Rebecca Hunt ❧ Santa Paula, CA

2 pounds Golden Delicious apples, peeled, cored and sliced into
½-inch wedges
2 tablespoons freshly squeezed lemon juice
½ cup plus 2 tablespoons sugar, divided
½ cup raisins
3½ tablespoons Calvados*, divided
1 teaspoon cinnamon
Rustic Tart Dough (recipe page 58)
3 tablespoons unsalted butter, cut into 6 to 8 pieces
1 cup apricot jam
Crème Chantilly (recipe page 58)

Calvados is an apple brandy. Any brandy or cognac will work in this recipe.

1. Preheat oven to 400°F. Toss apples with lemon juice in large bowl. Add ½ cup sugar, raisins, 2 tablespoons Calvados and cinnamon. Toss gently to mix; set aside.

2. Prepare Rustic Tart Dough.

3. Cut piece of parchment paper to fit 15×2-inch baking sheet or jelly-roll pan. Place paper on flat work surface and lightly flour. Remove pastry dough from refrigerator and place on parchment. Lightly flour top of dough. Roll out into 18×16-inch oval about ¼ inch thick. Transfer to baking sheet.

4. Pour apple mixture into center of dough, leaving 2-inch border free of filling along edges. Dot apple mixture with butter. Fold edges of dough up and over filling, overlapping as necessary. Press gently to seal seams (the center of the tart will remain open). Sprinkle edges with remaining 2 tablespoons sugar.

5. Bake 50 to 55 minutes or until tart dough is browned and apples are tender.

6. Meanwhile strain jam through fine sieve or stainer into small saucepan. Melt over low heat until jam becomes smooth; stir in remaining Calvados; keep warm. Brush warm tart with warm apricot mixutre. Serve with Crème Chantilly.   *Makes 8 servings*

continued on page 58

Rustic Apple Tart with Crème Chantilly, continued

Rustic Tart Crust

- 2 cups all-purpose flour
- 1 teaspoon sugar
- 1 teaspoon lemon zest
- ½ teaspoon salt
- ½ teaspoon cinnamon
- ½ cup vegetable shortening, chilled
- ½ cup unsalted cold butter, cut into ¼-inch dice
- ⅓ cup ice water

Place flour, sugar, lemon zest, salt and cinnamon in food processor; process using on/off pulsing action.

Add shortening and pulse 5 or 6 times to mix in. Add butter and pulse 8 to 10 times until dough resembles coarse crumbs. Add ice water and pulse just until dough begins to come together. Pour dough onto a piece of plastic cling wrap. Pat out into a 6-inch disk; seal in cling wrap and refrigerate at least 1 hour or overnight.

Crème Chantilly

- 1 cup heavy cream
- 1 tablespoon Calvados
- ½ to 1 tablespoon sugar

Whip cream in chilled medium bowl with chilled beaters just until beaters begin leaving tracks. With beaters running, add Calvados and sugar to taste. Continue whipping until soft peaks form. Refrigerate crème until ready to serve.

Hawaiian Paradise Pie

Patricia Harmon ❦ Baden, PA

1 unbaked (9-inch) pie crust
2 eggs, divided
½ cup coarsely chopped pecans
½ cup coarsely chopped macadamia nuts
⅓ cup corn syrup (blend half light corn syrup, half dark corn syrup)
1 can (21 ounces) pineapple pie filling
½ teaspoon cinnamon
1 package (8 ounces) cream cheese, softened
⅓ cup sugar
1 teaspoon vanilla
　Whipped Topping

1. Preheat oven to 375°F.

2. Beat 1 egg in medium bowl, then stir in pecans, macadamia nuts and corn syrup. Stir to combine, then pour into prepared pie crust. Bake 15 to 20 minutes or until partially set.

3. Meanwhile, combine pineapple pie filling and cinnamon in medium bowl; set aside. Beat cream cheese and sugar in medium bowl with electric mixer until fluffy. Add remaining egg and vanilla; beat until smooth.

4. Remove partially baked pie from oven and carefully spoon pineapple mixture on top of first layer. Spoon cream cheese layer on top of pineapple, spreading evenly to crust.

5. Return pie to oven and bake 20 to 25 minutes or until set. If necessary, cover crust only with foil during last 10 minutes to prevent overbrowning. Remove from oven and cool to room temperature. Refrigerate until chilled. Serve with whipped topping.　　　　　*Makes 8 to 10 servings*

Buttermilk Pie

Edna Ash ❧ Nashville, TN

1½ cups sugar
1 tablespoon cornstarch
½ cup buttermilk
½ cup butter, melted
3 eggs
1 tablespoon lemon juice
1 teaspoon vanilla
1 prepared (9-inch) graham cracker pie shell
Whipped cream (optional)

1. Preheat oven to 350°F.

2. Whisk together sugar and cornstarch in medium bowl. Mix in buttermilk, butter, eggs, lemon juice and vanilla. Beat with electric mixer on medium until smooth.

3. Pour into pie shell.

4. Bake 40 to 50 minutes or until set. Cool to room temperature and refrigerate. Serve chilled with whipped cream, if desired. *Makes 8 servings*

Lemon Meringue Pie

Catherine Gooch ❧ Colorado Springs, CO

1 baked (9-inch) deep dish pie crust
1 package (11 ounces) vanilla wafer cookies
1 can (13 ounces) sweetened condensed milk
½ cup lemon juice
2 eggs, separated
3 tablespoons marshmallow creme
Pinch of salt

1. Cover bottom of pie crust with vanilla wafers, reserving some for decoration.

2. Beat condensed milk, lemon juice and egg yolks with an electric mixer at low speed in top of 2-quart double boiler set over simmering water. Cook, beating constantly, until temperature reaches 160°F. Remove from heat.

3. Pour egg mixture into prepared pie crust, and decorate edge with reserved vanilla wafers. Cool to room temperature and refrigerate until ready to serve.

4. Just before serving, beat egg whites and marshmallow creme in medium bowl with electric mixer until stiff peaks form. Spoon onto pie, pulling up decorative peaks with tip of spoon. Bake in preheated 350°F oven until meringue is evenly brown. *Makes 8 servings*

Ganache-Topped Cheesecake

Carol Hartofil ❧ Farmingdale, NY

4 packages (8 ounces each) cream cheese, softened
1 pint heavy cream
7 eggs
1½ cups sugar
2 tablespoons all-purpose flour
2 teaspoons vanilla
Chocolate Ganache (recipe follows)

1. Preheat oven to 350°F. Beat cream cheese and cream in large bowl with electric mixer until smooth. Beat in eggs, one at a time, beating well after each addition. Add sugar, flour and vanilla; mix at low speed just until blended.

2. Pour mixture into ungreased 10-inch springform pan. Bake 1 hour or until center appears solid but still damp. Turn off oven but do not open door; allow to cool completely in oven for at least 4 hours. Prepare Chocolate Ganache.

3. Remove sides of springform pan and top with warm Chocolate Ganache, allowing chocolate to run down sides of cake. Cover and refrigerate 2 hours or until ready to serve.   *Makes 16 servings*

Chocolate Ganache: Heat 1 cup heavy cream in small saucepan over medium-low heat until bubbles appear around edges of pan. Place 1 cup semi-sweet chocolate chips in medium bowl. Pour cream over chips, stirring constantly until mixture is smooth and begins to thicken. Keep warm. Mixture thickens and sets as it cools.

Marty Ann's Famous Southern Pumpkin Cheesecake

Marty Ann Roark ❧ Las Vegas, NV

1¾ cups graham cracker crumbs
1 cup sugar, divided
½ cup butter or margarine, melted
1 package (8 ounces) cream cheese, softened
2 eggs, beaten
2 packages (3½ ounces each) French vanilla-flavored instant pudding mix
¾ cup milk
2 cups fresh pumpkin, mashed
⅛ teaspoon ground cinnamon
1 container (12 ounces) frozen whipped topping, thawed and divided
Dash nutmeg

1. Preheat oven to 350°F.

2. Combine cracker crumbs, ¼ cup sugar and butter in small bowl. Press into bottom of 9-inch springform pan. Set aside.

3. Beat cream cheese, eggs and remaining ¾ cup sugar in medium bowl with electric mixer at medium speed until fluffy. Spread over cracker crust. Bake 20 minutes; set aside to cool.

4. Combine pudding mix and milk in large bowl with electric mixer at medium speed 2 minutes. Add pumpkin and cinnamon; mix well. Stir in 1 cup whipped topping.

5. Spread pudding mixture over cream cheese layer. Spread remaining whipped topping over pudding layer. Sprinkle with nutmeg. Refrigerate 4 hours or overnight.   *Makes 12 to 15 servings*

Pineapple Cheesecake

Shirley Chancellor ❧ *Wichita Falls, TX*

1 package (3 ounces) lemon-flavored gelatin
1½ cups hot water
1 package (8 ounces) cream cheese, softened
1 cup sugar
½ cup milk
1 teaspoon vanilla
1 can (20 ounces) crushed pineapple, drained
1 container (8 ounces) frozen whipped topping, thawed
3 cups graham cracker crumbs
4 tablespoons powdered sugar
⅓ cup butter, melted

1. Dissolve gelatin in hot water in small bowl. Set aside to cool.

2. Beat cream cheese and sugar in large bowl with electric mixer at medium speed until creamy. Add milk and vanilla; beat until well combined. Add pineapple and gelatin mixture to cream cheese mixture. Fold in whipped topping. Set aside.

3. Combine cracker crumbs and powdered sugar in medium bowl. Add melted butter and mix until crumbly. Reserve 1¼ cups graham cracker mixture for topping. Spread remaining graham cracker mixture in 11×9-inch pan. Pat down firmly to form bottom crust.

4. Pour cream cheese mixture into pan. Sprinkle remaining 1¼ cups graham cracker mixture over top of cream cheese mixture.

5. Refrigerate 4 hours or until firmly set. *Makes 10 to 12 servings*

❧ Shirley says: ❧

Garnish the cheesecake with pineapple slices or maraschino cherries. Or, top with 1 can (20 ounces) cherry pie filling.

Root Beer Float Cheesecake

James Morrow ❧ Riverbank, CA

1½ cups shortbread cookie crumbs
2 tablespoons margarine, melted
4 packages (8 ounces each) cream cheese, softened
1 cup sugar
1 teaspoon vanilla
4 eggs
1½ teaspoons root beer concentrate
¼ cup plus 2 tablespoons powdered sugar
1½ cups whipping cream

Preheat oven to 350°F. Combine crumbs and margarine; press into bottom of 9-inch springform pan.

Beat cream cheese, sugar and vanilla in large bowl with electric mixer at medium speed until well blended. Add eggs; beat until blended.

Transfer 1¼ cups batter to small bowl. Add root beer concentrate; stir. Spoon half of plain cream cheese mixture into crust. Spoon half of root beer-flavored mixture over plain mixture. Repeat layers using plain and root beer mixtures. Swirl layers with knife or spatula to create marbled effect.

Bake 45 to 50 minutes or until center is almost set. Loosen cake from rim of pan; cool before removing, chill.

Beat whipping cream in large bowl with electric mixer at high speed until thickened, about 1½ minutes. (Chill bowl and beaters in freezer for best results.) Add powdered sugar. Beat at high speed until stiff peaks form, 1 to 2 minutes. Spread over cheesecake. Refrigerate until ready to serve.

Makes 10 to 12 servings

❧ James says: ❧

Substitute softened vanilla ice cream for whipped cream.

James Morrow

Chocolate Cheesecake

Shaun Efrole ❧ Rio Del, CA

8 squares (1 ounce each) semi-sweet or milk chocolate
3 tablespoons milk
1 tablespoon butter
8 to 10 chocolate wafers, crushed
3 cups buttermilk
1½ cups (12 ounces) cottage cheese
⅓ cup sugar
2½ packs (3 ounces) gelatin
¾ cup boiling water

1. Combine chocolate, milk and butter in medium saucepan. Melt over low heat, stirring occasionally. Add wafer crumbs. Pour chocolate mixture into 9-inch round cake pan.

2. Combine buttermilk, cottage cheese and sugar in medium bowl. Set aside.

3. Combine gelatin and water; stir until gelatin is dissolved. Cool. Add cottage cheese mixture to gelatin; mix well. Pour over chocolate crust in pan. Refrigerate 2 hours.

4. To serve, loosen cake from pan by placing bottom of pan in hot water at 5 second intervals. Invert pan onto serving plate. Garnish as desired.

Makes 8 servings

Low Carb Cream Cheese Dessert

Karen Drasler ❧ Sellsburg, IN

2 packages (8 ounces each) cream cheese, softened
2 teaspoons vanilla, divided
1 package (4-serving size) sugar-free lime-flavored gelatin
15 packets sugar substitute, divided
¾ cup hot water
2 cups heavy whipping cream, divided

Beat cream cheese and 1 teaspoon vanilla in large bowl with electric mixer. Combine gelatin and 11 packets sugar substitute in small bowl. Pour in hot water; stir until dissolved.

Add gelatin mixture to cream cheese mixture. Beat at low speed until well combined.

Beat 1 cup whipping cream in medium bowl until stiff peaks form. Add to cream cheese mixture. Beat at low speed. Pour mixture into 8×8-inch pan. Chill 2 hours.

Before serving, beat remaining 1 cup whipping cream, remaining 1 teaspoon vanilla and remaining 4 packets sugar substitute in medium bowl with electric mixer until stiff peaks form. Place dollop of whipped cream mixture on each serving of dessert. *Makes 8 servings*

❧ Karen says: ❧

You can substitute your favorite gelatin flavor for the lime gelatin.

Peanut Butter Cup Cheesecake

James Morrow Riverbank, CA

2 cups chocolate wafer crumbs
1/3 cup margarine, melted
2 packages (8 ounces each) cream cheese, softened and divided
3/4 cup plus 1 tablespoon sugar, divided
1/2 cup chunky style peanut butter
1 tablespoon plus 1 1/2 teaspoons all-purpose flour
3 eggs, divided
1/4 cup milk
2 squares (1 ounce each) semi-sweet chocolate, melted
1/8 teaspoon vanilla
    Miniature peanut butter cups, cut in half, for garnish (optional)

1. Preheat oven to 325°F.

2. Combine wafer crumbs and margarine in small bowl; press into bottom and up sides of 9-inch springform pan. Bake 10 minutes.

3. Combine 1 package cream cheese, 1/2 cup sugar, peanut butter and flour in large bowl. Beat with electric mixer at medium speed until well blended. (Batter will be very stiff.) Add 2 eggs, one at a time, beating well after each addition. Blend in milk. Pour cream cheese mixture evenly over crust.

4. *Increase oven temperature to 450°F.*

5. Beat remaining package cream cheese and remaining sugar in medium bowl with electric mixer at medium speed until well blended. Add remaining egg; mix well. Blend in chocolate and vanilla; spoon over peanut butter layer. Spread chocolate layer carefully to seal. Bake 10 minutes.

6. *Reduce oven temperature to 250°F.* Continue baking cheesecake 40 minutes.

7. Loosen cake from rim of pan; cool before removing. Chill. Garnish with peanut butter cups, if desired.   *Makes 10 to 12 servings*

Caramel Apple Cheesecake
LeeAnn Camut 🍓 Warrington, PA

1¼ cups graham cracker crumbs
¼ cup butter, melted
3 packages (8 ounces each) cream cheese, softened
¾ cup sugar
1½ teaspoons vanilla
3 eggs
1¼ cups apple pie filling
½ cup chopped peanuts
¼ cup caramel topping

1. Preheat oven to 350°F. Spray 9-inch springform pan with nonstick cooking spray.

2. Combine crumbs and butter in small bowl. Press into bottom of prepared pan. Bake 9 minutes; cool.

3. Beat cream cheese, sugar and vanilla in large bowl with electric mixer until well blended. Add eggs and beat well.

4. Pour cream cheese mixture over crust. Bake 40 to 50 minutes or until center is almost set. Refrigerate at least 3 hours. Carefully run knife around edge to loosen pan. Remove side of pan.

5. Spread apple filling over top of cake. Sprinkle peanuts over apple filling and drizzle with caramel topping. Serve immediately. Refrigerate leftovers.

Makes 12 servings

White Chocolate Pecan Caramel Cheesecake

Josephine Devereaux Piro ❧ *Easton, PA*

7 whole graham crackers
¼ cup butter, cut up
1 cup reduced-fat sour cream
4 eggs, separated
½ cup granulated sugar
1 tablespoon cornstarch
3 packages (8 ounces each) ⅓ less fat cream cheese
5 squares (1 ounce each) white baking chocolate, melted
2 tablespoons fresh lemon juice
2 teaspoons vanilla
2 tablespoons hot fudge ice cream topping
2 tablespoons caramel ice cream topping
½ cup coarsely chopped pecans
⅓ cup semi-sweet chocolate mini morsels

1. Preheat oven to 325°F. Grease 9-inch springform pan with nonstick cooking spray. Set aside.

2. Break graham crackers into food processor or blender; process with on/off pulses until finely crushed. Add butter; process with pulses until blended. Press crumb mixture into bottom and up sides of prepared pan. Set aside.

3. Beat sour cream, egg yolks, sugar and cornstarch in large bowl with electric mixer at medium speed until smooth. Add cream cheese, white chocolate, lemon juice and vanilla; beat until well blended.

4. Beat egg whites in large bowl until stiff peaks form. Fold in cream cheese mixture. Pour into prepared crust. Bake 15 minutes or until center jiggles slightly when shaken. Turn off oven and let cake cool 1 hour. Cool in pan on wire rack 10 minutes. Carefully run thin knife around edge of pan to release cake. Cool completely.

continued on page 74

Josephine Devereaux Piro

White Chocolate Pecan Caramel Cheesecake, continued

5. Remove sides of pan; place cheesecake on serving plate. Drizzle top with hot fudge and caramel ice cream toppings. Sprinkle with pecans and mini morsels. Cover and refrigerate 4 hours or overnight. Remove from refrigerator 1 hour before serving.   *Makes 12 to 16 servings*

Neapolitan Cheesecake

Lee Ann Camut ❧ Warrington, PA

1¼ cups chocolate wafer or graham cracker crumbs
¼ cup butter, melted
3 packages (8 ounces each) cream cheese, softened
¾ cup sugar
1½ teaspoons vanilla
3 eggs
⅓ cup strawberry preserves
6 drops red food coloring
¾ cup white chocolate chips, melted
¾ cup semi-sweet chocolate chips, melted

1. Preheat oven to 350°F. Spray 9-inch springform pan with cooking spray.

2. Combine crumbs and butter in medium bowl. Press into bottom of prepared pan. Bake 9 minutes; cool.

3. Beat cream cheese, sugar, and vanilla in large bowl with electric mixer at medium speed until well blended. Add eggs and beat well.

4. Divide batter equally into three medium bowls. Stir preserves and food coloring into one, white chocolate chips into second and semi-sweet chocolate chips into third. Pour semi-sweet chocolate mixture over crust; smooth with knife. Repeat with preserves mixture followed by white chocolate mixture.

5. Bake 1 hour or until center is almost set. Refrigerate at least 3 hours. Carefully run knife around edge of pan to loosen. Remove side of pan. Serve immediately. Refrigerate leftovers.   *Makes 8 to 10 servings*

Double Dutch Choco-Latte Cheesecake

LeeAnn Camut ❧ Warrington, PA

¼ cup butter, melted
2¾ teaspoons instant espresso powder or instant coffee, divided
1¼ cups chocolate wafer cookie crumbs
½ cup plus 2 tablespoons sugar, divided
2 packages (8 ounces each) cream cheese, softened
2 teaspoons vanilla
2 eggs
¼ cup unsweetened cocoa
¼ cup miniature semisweet chocolate chips
¼ cup chocolate-flavored syrup

1. Preheat oven to 350°F. Spray 9-inch springform pan with nonstick cooking spray.

2. Combine butter and 1½ teaspoons espresso powder in small bowl. Combine cookie crumbs and 2 tablespoons sugar in medium bowl. Add espresso mixture to cookie crumbs and stir until evenly combined. Press into bottom of prepared pan and bake 9 minutes. Remove to wire rack and cool in pan. *Reduce oven temperature to 325°F.*

3. Beat cream cheese, remaining ½ cup sugar and vanilla in large bowl with electric mixer at medium speed until well blended. Add 1 teaspoon espresso powder and eggs and beat until blended. Transfer half batter to another bowl and set aside. Add cocoa to remaining batter and beat at low speed until well blended. Pour over crust. Stir chocolate chips into reserved batter and pour over cocoa filling.

4. Bake 40 minutes or until center is almost set. Remove to wire rack and cool to room temperature. Cover and refrigerate for at least 3 hours or until ready to serve. Run thin knife around edge of pan before removing sides.

5. Heat chocolate syrup in microwave at HIGH 15 seconds. Stir in remaining ¼ teaspoon espresso powder. Drizzle sauce over slices of cake just before serving. *Makes 8 servings*

Lee Ann says:

I use the best quality Dutch process cocoa I can find. It makes a darker, richer cheesecake.

Butterscotch Bundt Cake

Valery Anderson ❧ Roseville, MI

1 package (18¼ ounces) yellow cake mix
1 package (4-serving size) butterscotch-flavored instant
  pudding mix
1 cup water
3 eggs
2 teaspoons cinnamon
½ cup chopped pecans
  Powdered sugar (optional)

Preheat oven to 325°F. Spray 10-inch Bundt pan with nonstick cooking spray. Combine all ingredients, except pecans and powdered sugar, in large bowl. Beat with electric mixer at medium-high speed 2 minutes. Stir in pecans. Pour into prepared pan. Bake 40 to 50 minutes or until cake springs back when lightly touched. Cool on wire rack 10 minutes. Invert cake on to serving plate. Cool completely. Sprinkle with powdered sugar, if desired.

Makes 10 to 12 servings

❧ Valery says: ❧

Try substituting white cake mix for yellow cake mix, pistachio-flavored pudding mix for butterscotch-flavored pudding mix and walnuts for pecans. It will make a delicious Pistachio Bundt Cake with Walnuts.

Banana Supreme Cake

Terrie Williams ❦ Franklinton, NC

1 package (18¼ ounces) yellow cake mix
1¼ cups water
3 large eggs
⅓ cup oil
1 teaspoon vanilla
   Vanilla Cream Cheese Icing (recipe page 79)
1 package (4-serving size) instant vanilla-flavored pudding mix
3 cups cold milk
3 large ripe bananas, sliced
1 cup lemon-lime-flavored soda
½ cup black walnut pieces, chopped

1. Preheat oven to 350°F. Grease and flour two 9-inch round cake pans. Set aside.

2. Beat cake mix, water, eggs, oil and vanilla in small bowl with electric mixer until smooth. Pour batter into prepared pans. Bake until golden or until toothpick inserted into centers of cakes is removed clean and dry.

3. Prepare Vanilla Cream Cheese Icing.

4. Combine pudding mix and milk. Beat until pudding begins to thicken. Refrigerate.

5. Soak sliced bananas in soda. After cake layers are completely cool, assemble cake. Place 1 cake layer on large serving platter. Top layer with half pudding mixture. Arrange sliced bananas in circular, overlapping pattern on top. Carefully spoon remaining pudding over sliced bananas. Top with second cake layer. Frost top and sides of cake with Vanilla Cream Cheese Icing. Garnish with black walnuts. Refrigerate until ready to serve.   *Makes 8 to 10 servings*

Vanilla Cream Cheese Icing

2 containers (8 ounces each) frozen whipped topping, thawed
1 package (8 ounces) cream cheese, softened
3 tablespoons boiling water
2 tablespoons powdered sugar
1 teaspoon vanilla extract

Combine all ingredients in large bowl and beat with electric mixer at medium speed until creamy and smooth.

Pineapple Coconut Poundcake

Brenda B. Melancon ❧ Bay St. Louis, MS

1 package (18¼ ounces) yellow cake mix
1 package (4-serving size) cheesecake-flavored instant pudding mix
1 can (8 ounces) crushed pineapple, undrained
3 eggs
½ cup water
¼ cup vegetable oil
1 cup shredded coconut
   Non-dairy whipped topping (optional)

Preheat oven to 350°F. Grease two 8×4×2-inch loaf pans. Combine all ingredients except coconut and whipped topping in large bowl. Beat at medium speed with electric mixer 2 minutes. Stir in coconut. Pour into prepared pans. Bake 45 to 50 minutes or until toothpick inserted into centers comes out clean. Cool 10 minutes in pans; remove to wire racks. Serve with whipped topping, if desired.   *Makes 24 servings*

Chocolate-Raspberry Layer Cake

Janel M. Belbute ❧ Haverhill, MA

2 packages (18¼ ounces each) chocolate cake mix, plus ingredients to
    prepare
1 container (16 ounces) chocolate frosting
1 jar (10 ounces) seedless raspberry fruit spread, divided
1 package (12 ounces) white chocolate chips, divided
½ pint fresh raspberries, divided
1 to 2 cups toasted sliced almonds

1. Preheat oven to 350°F. Grease and flour four 9-inch round cake pans.
Prepare cake according to package directions. Pour into prepared pans. Bake as
directed on package. Cool completely.

2. Place one cake layer on decorative serving tray. Spread ⅓ of fruit preserves
on top of cake. Sprinkle with ½ cup white chocolate chips. Repeat with second
and third layers, fruit spread and white chocolate chips.

3. Place fourth cake layer on top. Frost top and sides of cake with chocolate
frosting. Decorate cake in alternating concentric circles of raspberries and
remaining ½ cup white chocolate chips. Press almonds against side of cake.

Makes 8 to 10 servings

Delicious Strawberry Cake

Alexis Hitchman ❧ Butler, OH

> 4 eggs, separated
> 1 package (18¼ ounces) yellow cake mix
> 1⅓ cups milk
> 1 package (4-serving size) vanilla-flavored instant pudding mix
> ¼ cup oil
> 1 teaspoon vanilla
> Icing (recipe page 83)
> 1 quart strawberries, stemmed and halved

1. Preheat oven to 375°F. Grease and flour two 9-inch round cake pans. Set aside.

2. Beat egg whites in medium bowl with electric mixer at medium speed until soft peaks form; set aside. Combine all remaining ingredients, except Icing and strawberries, in large bowl. Fold in egg whites.

3. Pour half of batter into each prepared pan. Bake 28 to 32 minutes or until toothpick inserted into centers comes out clean.

4. Cool cakes 15 minutes in pans. Remove from pans and cool completely on wire racks.

5. Prepare Icing. Refrigerate until ready to use.

6. Cut cakes in half horizontally to make four layers. Place one layer on serving plate. Spread Icing over layer and top with strawberries. Repeat with remaining three cake layers, Icing and strawberries. Frost top layer and sides of cake with remaining Icing. Garnish with remaining strawberries.

Makes 10 to 12 servings

Icing

1 package (8 ounces) cream cheese, softened
1 container (8 ounces) frozen whipped topping, thawed
1 cup granulated sugar
1 cup powdered sugar
4 tablespoons margarine, softened
1 teaspoon vanilla

Combine all ingredients in small bowl. Beat with electric mixer at medium speed until smooth.

Coconut Pineapple Cake

June Pittman 🍓 LaGrange, GA

1 package (18¼ ounces) yellow cake mix
1½ cups milk
5 eggs
½ cup vegetable oil
1 teaspoon coconut extract
1 teaspoon pineapple extract
1 can (14 ounces) sweetened condensed milk
2 packages (7 ounces each) shredded coconut
1 can (20 ounces) crushed pineapple
1 cup chopped marashino cherries, drained

Preheat oven to 325°F. Grease 13×9-inch pan.

Combine cake mix, milk, eggs, oil, coconut and pineapple extracts in large bowl. Pour batter into prepared pan. Bake 40 to 45 minutes or until toothpick inserted into center comes out clean. Cool.

Combine condensed milk and 1 package coconut in small bowl; mix well.

Drain pineapple, reserving ¼ cup juice. Discard remaining juice. Add pineapple to coconut mixture; mix well.

Poke holes in cake using tines of fork. Pour reserved ¼ cup pineapple juice over cake. Spread pineapple mixture over cake. Sprinkle remaining package coconut and cherries over cake. Cut in squares to serve. Refrigerate leftovers.

Makes 10 to 12 servings

Chocolate Rum Cake

Tricia Bailey ✣ Moody, AL

1 cup chopped pecans
1 package (12 ounces) semi-sweet chocolate chips
1 package (8 ounces) cream cheese, softened
1 package (18¼ ounces) yellow cake mix
1 package (4-serving size) vanilla-flavored instant pudding mix
5 eggs
½ cup oil
½ cup cold water
3 tablespoons dark rum
1 teaspoon vanilla
Rum Butter Glaze (recipe follows)

1. Preheat oven to 325°F. Grease and flour 10-inch tube pan or 12-cup Bundt pan. Sprinkle chopped pecans evenly across bottom of pan.

2. Place chocolate chips and cream cheese in microwavable glass bowl. Melt in microwave at MEDIUM (50% power) 1 minute. Stir unitl smooth and set aside to cool.

3. Combine cake mix, pudding mix, eggs, oil, water, rum and vanilla in large bowl; mix until smooth. Add chocolate mixture and blend.

4. Pour batter into prepared pan. Bake 45 to 50 minutes or until toothpick inserted near center of cake is removed clean. *Do not overbake.* Cool in pan 15 minutes.

5. Prepare Rum Butter Glaze.

6. Spoon ½ glaze over cake while cake in still in pan. Invert cake onto serving platter. Brush remaining glaze over top and sides of cake. Wrap tightly in aluminum foil until ready to serve. *Makes 10 to 12 servings*

Rum Butter Glaze

½ cup butter
1 cup sugar
¼ cup water
3 tablespoons dark rum
1 teaspoon vanilla

Melt butter in medium saucepan over low heat. Add sugar and water and boil 5 minutes, stirring often. Remove syrup from heat and let cool. Stir in rum and vanilla.

Tricia says:

For best flavor, leave cake wrapped in foil for at least 24 hours before serving. You may warm the cake slices and serve with a scoop of chocolate or rum raisin ice cream!

Red Velvet Cake

Lynette Hacker Richmond, CA

2 packages (18¼ ounces each) white cake mix
2 teaspoons baking soda
3 cups buttermilk
4 eggs
2 bottles (1 ounce each) red food coloring
1 container (16 ounces) vanilla frosting

1. Preheat oven to 350°F. Grease and flour four 9-inch round cake pans. Set aside.

2. Combine cake mixes and baking soda in large bowl. Add buttermilk, eggs and food coloring. Beat with electric mixer at low speed until moistened. Beat at high 2 minutes.

3. Pour batter into prepared pans. Bake 30 to 35 minutes or until toothpick inserted into centers comes out clean. Cool 10 minutes. Remove cakes from pans to wire rack and cool completely.

4. To assemble cake, place one cake layer on serving plate. Spread frosting evenly over layer. Carefully place second layer on top and frost. Repeat with third and fourth layers. Frost top and sides of cake.   *Makes 10 servings*

Creamy Coconut Cake with Almond Filling

Donna Myers ❧ Lewisville, NC

1 package (18¼ ounces) white cake mix
3 eggs
1 cup sour cream
½ cup vegetable oil
1 teaspoon vanilla
1 teaspoon coconut flavoring
1 can (12½ ounces) prepared almond filling
2 cans (16 ounces each) prepared creamy coconut frosting
½ cup sliced almonds

1. Preheat oven to 350°F. Spray two (9-inch) round pans lightly with nonstick cooking spray and dust with 1 teaspoon flour. Tap pans to remove excess flour.

2. Combine cake mix, eggs, sour cream, oil, vanilla and coconut flavoring in large bowl. Beat with electric mixer at low speed for 1 minute. Scrape sides of bowl with rubber spatula; beat 2 minutes. Divide evenly between prepared pans. Bake until golden brown or until toothpick inserted into centers of cake is clean and dry when removed. Cool in pans on wire racks.

3. When cakes are completely cool, turn out onto cutting board and slice horizontally in half, creating 4 equal layers. Place one layer cut side down on serving plate and spread with ½ almond filling. Top with second layer of cake and spread top with ½ cup coconut frosting. Top with third layer and spread with remaining almond filling. Top with fourth cake layer and spread remaining coconut frosting evenly over top and sides of cake. Sprinkle cake with sliced almonds. *Makes 8 to 12 servings*

❧ Donna says: ❧

Can be stored at room temperature, but I prefer to keep it refrigerated until ready to serve.

Creamy Coconut Cake with Almond Filling

Pumpkin Spice Cake

Carol Hale ❧ Paris, OH

1 package (18¼ ounces) spice cake mix
1 can (15 ounces) pumpkin
  Powdered sugar

Preheat oven to 350°F. Grease 13×9-inch pan. Set aside. Combine cake mix and pumpkin in medium bowl; mix well. Mixture will be thick. Pour batter into prepared pan. Bake 30 to 35 minutes or until toothpick inserted into center comes out clean. Cool completely. Sprinkle with powdered sugar.

Makes 10 to 12 servings

Pineapple-Coconut Cake

Peggy M. Gill ❧ Allendale, SC

1 package (18¼ ounces) butter cake mix
¾ cup milk
½ cup butter
3 eggs
½ teaspoon vanilla
1 can (20 ounces) crushed pineapple in heavy syrup, undrained
1 cup sugar
1 teaspoon cornstarch
1 container (8 ounces) sour cream
2 cups fresh coconut, shredded
1 teaspoon coconut extract

Preheat oven to 325°F.

Combine cake mix, milk, butter, eggs and vanilla in large bowl. Pour batter into two 8-inch round cake pans.

Bake 25 to 30 minutes or until toothpick inserted into centers comes out clean.

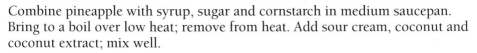

Combine pineapple with syrup, sugar and cornstarch in medium saucepan. Bring to a boil over low heat; remove from heat. Add sour cream, coconut and coconut extract; mix well.

Place one cake layer on serving plate. Spread coconut mixture on top of cake. Place remaining cake layer over coconut mixture. Spread top and sides of cake with coconut mixture. Refrigerate until ready to serve.   *Makes 10 servings*

Angel Food Cake Roll

Tammy J. Christiansen ❦ *Dixon, IL*

> 1 package (16 ounces) angel food cake mix, plus ingredients to
>   prepare cake
> ¼ cup plus 2 tablespoons powdered sugar
> 1 cup cold milk
> 1 package (4-serving size) vanilla-flavored instant pudding mix
> 1 cup whipping cream

Preheat oven 350°F.

Line bottom of 15×10-inch jelly-roll pan with waxed paper. Prepare cake mix according to package directions. Bake 20 minutes or until cake is golden brown and springs back when lightly touched. Cool on wire rack 15 minutes. Lay clean towel on flat surface. Sift ¼ cup powdered sugar over towel. Invert cake on top of sugar. Carefully peel off waxed paper. Starting at short end of cake, roll up with towel, jelly-roll style. Cool 30 minutes, seam side down, on wire rack.

Beat milk and pudding mix in large bowl with electric mixer at low speed 2 minutes. Let stand 5 minutes. Beat whipping cream in separate bowl with electric mixer at high speed until soft peaks form. Fold whipped cream into pudding mixture.

Unroll cake. Spread filling to within 1 inch of edge of cake. Reroll and place, seam side down, on serving plate. Dust with remaining 2 tablespoons powdered sugar.   *Makes 8 servings*

Five Layer Brownie Dessert

Janine Stidley ❧ Savannah, GA

1 package (19 to 21 ounces) chocolate brownie mix, plus ingredients
    to prepare

1 package (4-serving size) chocolate-flavored instant pudding mix,
    plus ingredients to prepare

1 package (8 ounces) cream cheese, softened

4 to 5 cups powdered sugar

2 cups (12 ounces) milk chocolate chips, divided

1 container (8 ounces) frozen whipped topping, thawed

1. Prepare brownie mix according to package directions for 13×9-inch pan.
Set aside.

2. Prepare pudding mix according to package directions.

3. Combine cream cheese and powdered sugar in medium bowl. Set aside.

4. Sprinkle prepared brownie with 1½ cups chocolate chips. Evenly spread
cream cheese mixture over chocolate chips. Spread pudding mixture over
cream cheese mixture. Spread whipped topping over pudding mixture.
Sprinkle remaining ½ cup chocolate chips over whipped topping. Refrigerate
until ready to serve. *Makes 12 to 14 servings*

Prep 10 minutes plus standing
Cook 5 minutes
Makes 8 servings

8 c. cold water
8 tea bags, tags removed
8 fresh sprigs mint plus
  additional for serving
¼ c. fresh lime juice
  (from 2 or 3 limes)
  Ice cubes
  Superfine sugar (optional)

1. In covered 3-quart saucepan, heat
cups water to boiling over high hea
Remove from heat; stir in tea bags a
mint. Cover and let steep 5 minutes.
2. Stir tea; remove tea bags and mi
Into large pitcher with tight-fitting
pour tea, lime juice, and remainin
cups water. Makes 6½ cups. Cover
let stand until ready to serve or o
night. (Do not refrigerate or tea wil
come cloudy. If this happens, add u
1 cup boiling water, gradually, sti
until tea clears.) Serve over ice
mint, and sugar if you like.

Minty Iced Tea
(also pictured on page 148)

ReciTip Superfine sugar is a finer ver-
sion of granulated sugar. Although it's
available at most supermarkets, you can
make your own by pulsing granulated
sugar in a blender or processor until the
crystals are more powder-like. Confec-
tioners' sugar (which contains some
cornstarch) is not a good substitute.

EACH SERVING About 5 calories, 0 g
protein, 1 g carbohydrate, 0 g total fat
fiber, 0 mg cholesterol, 5 mg sodium.

him! *Please, will you read this for me?* [*Laughs*]

LS: Looking back over your lengthy body of work, I was surprised to see how often you've played really intense roles, parts that aren't actually all that glamorous.

MP: Well, I find it interesting that I have done very few films where I've actually wanted to keep my wardrobe. So that sort of sums up a lot of the roles I've played.

LS: But I do think of you as a leading lady in the traditional sense. And you've worked opposite some incredible leading men—Jack Nicholson, Al Pacino, Sean Penn, Mel Gibson, George Clooney....

MP: Yeah, it's a pretty impressive list. I've been so lucky, haven't I? And now I've been up against John Travolta in drag!

How do you feel about that?

MP: Well, I had so much fun, and the critics may accuse me of chewing up the scenery, of overacting, and that will be fine, because that's sort of what I needed to do. And to do that, I did have to leave my comfort zone.

LS: Growing up, did you always know you wanted to act?

MP: You know, I did, but it was more of a kid's fantasy than something that seemed really achievable, like a realistic goal. When I went into it, as a young woman, I thought the chances of succeeding were so ridiculously small that my philosophy was, Well, I'll give this a shot and if I don't succeed, I'm still young enough to figure out something else to do. I actually went to school to be a court reporter for a little while.

LS: Lucky for us that didn't work out! You once famously said that being considered "too pretty" kept you

Pineapple Delight

Tammy Reigle ❧ Moncks Corner, SC

1 package (18¼ ounces) pineapple cake mix, plus ingredients to
   prepare
2 packages (4-serving size) vanilla-flavored instant pudding mix
3 cups milk
1 cup powdered sugar
1 container (8 ounces) frozen whipped topping, thawed
1 can (20 ounces) pineapple chunks, drained

Bake cake according to package directions for 11×8-inch pan. Cool
completely. Combine pudding mix, milk, powdered sugar and whipped
topping in medium bowl. Set aside. Cut cake in half and crumble one half into
large bowl. Spread pudding mixture over top of crumbled cake. Spread half of
pineapple over pudding mixture. Repeat layers starting with remaining half of
cake ending with pineapple. Chill in refrigerator 3 to 4 hours.

Makes 10 servings

Apple Spice Cake

Lorinda Platti ❧ Germantown, NY

1 can (21 ounces) apple pie filling
1 package (about 18 ounces) moist spice cake mix
3 teaspoons ground cinnamon, divided
3 eggs, lightly beaten
6 ounces cream cheese

1. Preheat oven to 350°F. Grease and flour 12-cup Bundt pan or 10-inch
tube pan.

2. Place pie filling in large bowl. Chop apples into ¼-inch bits with small
knife or mash with potato masher (filling should be lumpy, not puréed). Add
cake mix, 2 teaspoons cinnamon and eggs to pie filling. Beat 30 seconds with
electric mixer at low speed. Scrape sides of bowl; beat 2 minutes more on high
speed. Pour into prepared pan and bake 45 to 55 minutes or until toothpick
inserted near center of cake comes out clean.

3. Cool in pan 1 hour. Invert onto serving plate. Place cream cheese in small saucepan over low heat, stirring frequently until smooth. Stir in remaining cinnamon, then drizzle over cake.   *Makes 12 servings*

Butter Brickle Cake

Marci Carl ❧ Northern Cambria, PA

⅔ cup sugar

2 teaspoons cinnamon

1 package (about 18 ounces) yellow cake mix

1 package (4-serving size) butterscotch-flavored instant pudding mix

4 eggs

¾ cup oil

¾ cup water

1 cup chopped walnuts, divided

1. Preheat oven to 350°F. Grease and flour 13×9-inch cake pan. Combine sugar and cinnamon in small bowl; set aside.

2. Combine cake mix, pudding mix, eggs, oil and water in large bowl. Beat with electric mixer 4 to 5 minutes or until batter is fluffy; scrape sides of bowl. Pour ½ cake batter into prepared pan. Sprinkle ½ cup walnuts evenly on top. Sprinkle with half cinnamon-sugar mixture. Cover with remaining cake batter. Sprinkle remaining walnuts into batter. Sprinkle with remaining cinnamon-sugar mixture.

3. Bake 40 to 45 minutes or until toothpick inserted into center of cake is clean when removed. Cool in pan.   *Makes 12 to 15 servings*

❧ Marci says: ❧

This cake is great served warm from the oven, topped with whipped cream or partially melted vanilla ice cream!

Grandma's Favorites

Lemon Cheese Bars
April Hart ❧ Leon, WV

1 package (about 18 ounces) white or yellow cake mix
  with pudding in the mix
2 eggs, divided
⅓ cup vegetable oil
1 package (8 ounces) cream cheese
⅓ cup sugar
1 teaspoon lemon juice

1. Preheat oven to 350°F.

2. Combine cake mix, 1 egg and oil in large bowl until crumbly.
Press cake mixture into ungreased 13×9-inch cake pan, reserving
1 cup mixture. Bake 15 minutes or until light golden brown.

3. Beat remaining egg, cream cheese, sugar and lemon juice until
light in color and smooth. Spread over baked layer. Sprinkle with
reserved cake mixture. Bake 15 minutes longer. Cool in pan on
wire rack; cut into bars.   *Makes 18 bars*

Mom's Apple Crisp
Kim Carroll ❧ Hastings, MN

4 cups Granny Smith apples, peeled and thinly sliced
½ cup granulated sugar
½ cup plus 1 tablespoon all-purpose flour, divided
½ teaspoon cinnamon
½ cup quick-cooking oats
½ cup brown sugar
½ teaspoon baking soda
¼ teaspoon salt
⅛ teaspoon baking powder
¼ cup butter, softened
    Vanilla ice cream (optional)

Preheat oven to 350°F. Spray 9×9-inch baking dish with nonstick cooking spray. Set aside. Combine apples, sugar, 1 tablespoon flour and cinnamon in large bowl. Pour into prepared pan. Combine remaining ½ cup flour, oats, brown sugar, baking soda, salt and baking powder in large bowl. Cut in butter with pasty blender or two knives. Blend until mixture resembles coarse crumbs. Sprinkle over apple mixture. Bake, uncovered, 35 minutes or until hot and bubbly. Serve warm with ice cream, if desired.   *Makes 4 servings*

Sunshine Cake

Theresa Brousil Burbank, IL

12 eggs, separated
$\frac{1}{8}$ teaspoon salt
1 teaspoon cream of tartar
1$\frac{1}{4}$ cups granulated sugar
1 cup cake flour
1 teaspoon vanilla
Butter Custard Icing (recipe follows)
Toasted coconut (optional)
Chopped nuts (optional)

1. Preheat oven 350°F.

2. Beat 9 egg yolks in large bowl with electric mixer until thick.

3. Beat 1$\frac{1}{2}$ cups egg whites and salt in separate large bowl with electric mixer until foamy. (Save remaining 2 egg yolks for Butter Custard Icing; discard remaining yolks.) Add cream of tartar and beat until almost stiff. Add sugar.

4. Fold egg yolks into egg white mixture; add flour and vanilla. Pour batter into 10-inch tube pan. Cut through batter with knife to release air.

5. Bake 1 hour or until cake springs back when lightly touched.

6. Prepare Butter Custard Icing.

7. Invert cake onto serving plate. Spread frosting over cake. Top with toasted coconut and chopped nuts, if desired.   *Makes 12 servings*

Butter Custard Icing

$\frac{1}{2}$ cup milk
$\frac{1}{2}$ cup powdered sugar
2 egg yolks (reserved from cake)
$\frac{1}{2}$ cup butter

Scald milk in top of double boiler. Combine powder sugar and egg yolks in small bowl. Add about 2 tablespoons milk to egg mixture. Add mixture to remaining milk. Heat in double boiler until thick like custard. Cool over bowl filled with cold water. Beat butter in medium bowl with electric mixture. Add custard. Beat until well combined.

California Gold Rush Rice Pudding

Lois Dowling ❧ Tacoma, WA

1 cup arborio rice
2 cans (12 ounces each) orange soda
½ cup diced dried apricots
1 teaspoon butter
¼ teaspoon salt
½ cup chopped dates
⅓ cup toasted sliced honey roasted almonds
3 cups frozen whipped topping, thawed

Combine rice, soda, apricots, butter and salt in large saucepan with a tight-fitting lid. Bring to boil over medium-high heat, stirring frequently. Reduce heat to low and cover tightly. Simmer 25 to 30 minutes or until liquid is absorbed. Remove from heat and cool. Fold in dates and almonds. Refrigerate until ready to serve. Top with whipped topping before serving.

Makes 6 servings

Ambrosia

Laura Fitzgerald ❧ New City, NY

1 package (4-serving size) gelatin, any flavor, plus ingredients to prepare
1 can (20 ounces) crushed pineapple, undrained
1 can (11 ounces) mandarin oranges, undrained
2 cups sour cream
½ cup shredded coconut
1 cup miniature marshmallows

Prepare gelatin according to package directions substituting juice from pineapple and oranges for cold water. Add sour cream to gelatin; whisk until smooth. Stir in fruit and coconut. Top with marshmallows. Refrigerate until firm.

Makes 8 to 10 servings

Apple Pita

Emily Hale 🌿 *Chicago, IL*

½ cup sugar
1 tablespoon cornstarch
1 teaspoon cinnamon
5 medium macintosh apples, peeled and chopped
¾ cup butter
1 package (16 ounces) frozen phyllo dough, thawed
    Vanilla ice cream (optional)

Preheat oven to 350°F. Grease 15×10-inch baking dish. Set aside.

Combine sugar, cornstarch and cinnamon in large bowl. Add apples and toss to coat.

Melt butter in microwave-safe dish in 30 second increments until completely melted.

Unroll phyllo dough and place underneath damp towel. Place 1 sheet phyllo dough in prepared dish. Using pastry brush, lightly coat phyllo dough with melted butter. Continue using 3 more sheets of phyllo dough and brushing melted butter on top of each sheet. Place apple mixture on top of layered phyllo. Continue to layer phyllo dough and melted butter on top of apple mixture to make 4 more layers.

Bake 40 minutes or until golden brown. Serve warm with ice cream, if desired.

Makes 10 to 12 servings

Helpful Hint

Unopened packages of phyllo dough will keep in the refrigerator up to one month and frozen up to one year. Thaw frozen dough in the refrigerator overnight. Thawed and opened packages, if wrapped securely, will keep in the refrigerator two to three days.

Caramel Apple Bread Pudding with Cinnamon Cream

Beth Royals 🌿 *Richmand, VA*

1 package (12 ounces) frozen escalloped apples, thawed
8 eggs, lightly beaten
2 cups milk
2 cups half-and-half
1 cup granulated sugar
½ cup unsalted butter, melted
2 teaspoons baking powder
1½ teaspoon ground cinnamon, divided
1 teaspoon vanilla
1 loaf (16 ounces) challah or any sweet bread, cut into ¾-inch cubes
1 package (12¼ ounces) caramel ice cream topping
2 cup vanilla ice cream
Additional vanilla ice cream (optional)
Mint sprigs (optional)

1. Preheat oven to 350°F. Spray 13×9-inch baking pan with nonstick cooking spray.

2. Combine apples, eggs, milk, half-and-half, sugar, butter, baking powder, 1 teaspoon cinnamon and vanilla in large bowl. Mix well. Gently fold in bread cubes. Pour into prepared pan.

3. Bake 50 minutes. Cool in pan 20 minutes.

4. Drizzle ½ cup caramel topping over bread pudding. Cut into 16 sections.

5. Microwave ice cream in small bowl about 30 seconds or until partially melted. Stir until smooth. Add remaining ½ teaspoon cinnamon and whisk until combined. Place ⅛ of sauce on each serving plate. Top with serving of bread pudding. Drizzle each serving with ¼ cup caramel topping. Top with ice cream and mint sprig, if desired.   *Makes 16 servings*

Banana-Nut Cake with Brown Sugar Topping

Carol Wright ❧ Cartersville, GA

Cake

3 bananas, mashed
1½ cups brown sugar, divided
1½ cups all-purpose flour
1 cup nuts
½ cup white chocolate chips
½ cup oil
1 egg
¼ cup milk
1 teaspoon baking soda

Topping

1⅔ cups brown sugar
½ cup butter
½ cup nuts

Preheat oven to 350°F. Grease and flour 1-quart casserole or soufflé dish. Set aside. Combine all cake ingredient in large bowl. Pour into prepared dish. Bake 30 to 35 minutes. Meanwhile, combine 1⅔ cups brown sugar and butter in medium saucepan. Heat over medium heat until sugar dissolves and mixture is smooth. Remove cake from oven. Immediately sprinkle with nuts and pour brown sugar mixture over cake. *Makes 4 servings*

Grandma's Chamtorte Dessert

Catherine Reiter ❧ Altoon, WI

6 egg whites
2 cups sugar
1 teaspoon vanilla
1 teaspoon vinegar
1 pint whipping cream
2 tablespoons powdered sugar
1 can (20 ounces) crushed pineapple, well-drained
   Chopped pecans (optional)

Preheat oven to 325°F. Grease two 9-inch round cake pans. Line pans with greased waxed paper. Set aside.

Beat egg whites in large bowl with electric mixer at medium speed until stiff peaks form. Gradually beat in sugar. Add vanilla and vinegar. Stir until combined.

Pour into prepared pans. Bake 1 hour or until dry. Carefully remove tortes from pans while warm. Cool completely on wire racks. Remove wax paper. Beat whipping cream in large bowl until stiff. Gradually add powdered sugar; stir in pineapple. Place one torte layer on serving plate. Frost with whipping cream mixture. Repeat with second layer. Sprinkle with pecans, if desired. Serve immediately or refrigerate for up to 1 day.   *Makes 8 servings*

Date-Nut Orange Bars

Lina Jusell 🍃 Port Angeles, WA

¾ cup all-purpose flour
½ teaspoon baking powder
½ teaspoon salt
1 cup brown sugar
¼ cup shortening, melted and cooled
2 eggs, well-beaten
1 cup chopped dates
1 cup pecans
1 cup chopped orange wedge gel candies
Powdered sugar, for garnish

1. Preheat oven to 350°F. Grease 8×8-inch square baking pan. Set aside. Sift flour, baking powder and salt twice into large bowl. Add brown sugar; mix well. Combine shortening and eggs in small bowl. Add to flour mixture. Stir in dates, pecans and gel candies.

2. Bake 25 to 30 minutes or until toothpick inserted into center comes out clean. Cut into bars while still hot. Cool; dust with powdered sugar.

Makes 16 bars

Baked Custard

Helen Fan 🍃 Cupertino, CA

3 eggs, slightly beaten
⅓ cup sugar
1 teaspoon vanilla
⅛ teaspoon salt
2½ cups milk, scalded
Nutmeg

Preheat oven to 350°F. Combine eggs, sugar, vanilla and salt in medium bowl. Stir in milk. Pour into six 6-ounce custard cups. Sprinkle each cup with nutmeg. Place cups in 13×9×2-inch baking dish. Pour very hot water into pan within ½ inch of tops of cups. Bake 45 minutes or until knife inserted halfway between center and edge comes out clean. Serve warm or chilled. Refrigerate any remaining custard.

Makes six (6-ounce) servings

Lemony Layers

Constance McMorris ❧ *Newberry, SC*

3 eggs, separated
1 cup sugar
½ cup milk
¼ cup all-purpose flour
4 tablespoons lemon juice
2 tablespoons butter, melted
Whipped cream (optional)

1. Preheat oven to 350°F.

2. Beat egg yolks in large bowl with electric mixer at medium speed until light and fluffy. Add sugar, milk, flour and lemon juice. Beat until smooth. Fold in butter.

3. Beat egg whites in medium bowl until stiff peaks form. Fold into egg yolk mixture.

4. Pour into a 1½ quart casserole dish. Bake 40 minutes or until top is lightly browned. Top with whipped cream, if desired. Serve warm or cold.

Makes 6 to 8 servings

Vinegar Stew

Gracie Hardymon ❧ *Charlottesville, IN*

2 egg yolks
2 tablespoons plus 1 teaspoon sugar
4 tablespoons vinegar
⅛ teaspoon dash salt
1½ pounds seedless grapes
5 bananas, sliced

Combine all ingredients except grapes and bananas in medium saucepan. Heat over low heat until thick, stirring constantly. Place grapes and banana slices into individual serving bowls. Top fruit with Vinegar Stew.

Makes 4 servings

Zucchini and Apple Pound Cake
Jean Jackson 🪰 Columbus, GA

2¾ cups sugar
2¼ cups unsalted butter
 5 eggs
⅓ cup applesauce
¼ cup grated zucchini
½ cup evaporated milk
 3 cups all-purpose flour
1½ teaspoon baking powder
½ teaspoon baking soda
⅛ teaspoon salt
 2 teaspoons vanilla
½ medium Golden Delicious apple, cored and diced
 1 teaspoon lemon juice
  Zucchini and Apple Frosting (recipe follows)
  Vanilla ice cream (optional)

1. Preheat oven to 350°F. Grease 10-inch tube baking pan. Set aside.

2. Beat sugar and butter in large bowl with electric mixer until pale and fluffy. Add eggs, one at a time, beating well after each addition. Mix in applesauce and zucchini.

3. Stir in evaporated milk, mixing well. Beat 2 minutes, scraping sides and bottom of bowl. Combine flour, baking powder, baking soda and salt in large bowl. Add to butter mixture; mix well. Stir in vanilla, apple and lemon juice.

4. Pour batter into prepared pan. Bake 75 to 80 minutes or until toothpick inserted near center comes out clean. Remove from oven and cool in pan 15 minutes. When cake is cool, invert onto serving plate. Frost with Zucchini and Apple Frosting. Serve with vanilla ice cream, if desired.

Makes 10 servings

Zucchini and Apple Frosting

1 package (16 ounces) powdered sugar
1 package (8 ounces) cream cheese
½ cup butter
1 teaspoon vanilla
4 to 6 tablespoons milk
⅓ cup finely grated zucchini
½ Golden Delicious apple, diced

1. Beat sugar, cream cheese, butter and vanilla in medium bowl with electric mixer until fluffy.

2. Add 2 tablespoons milk; fold in zucchini and apple. Stir well. If frosting seems too thick, add more milk, one tablespoon at a time, until frosting is of spreading consistency.

Noodle Pudding

Laura Fitzgerald ❧ New City, NY

4 cups ricotta cheese
2 cups sour cream
1½ cups granulated sugar
8 eggs
1 can (20 ounces) crushed pineapple, drained
1 teaspoon vanilla
1 package (10 ounces) egg noodles, cooked and drained

Preheat oven to 350°F. Grease 13×9-inch baking dish. Set aside. Combine ricotta cheese, sour cream, sugar, eggs, pineapple and vanilla in large bowl. Fold in noodles. Pour into prepared pan. Cover with foil. Bake 1 hour.

Makes 12 to 14 servings

Moist and Tender Carrot Cake

Lina Jusell 🌿 Port Angeles, WA

2 cups granulated sugar

1½ cups vegetable oil

1 teaspoon vanilla

2½ cups all-purpose flour

2 tablespoon ground cinnamon, divided

1 teaspoon baking soda

1 teaspoon salt

½ teaspoon ground ginger

4 eggs

2 cups grated carrots

1 cup canned crushed pineapple, drained and juice reserved

¾ cup chopped pecans

½ cup golden raisins

Pineapple juice

Cream Cheese Frosting (recipe follows)

1. Preheat oven to 350°F. Grease and flour two 8-inch round cake pans. Set aside.

2. Combine sugar, oil and vanilla in large bowl. Sift flour, 1 tablespoon cinnamon, baking soda, salt and ginger into medium bowl. Add flour mixture to sugar mixture, alternating with eggs. Add carrots, pineapple, pecans and raisins; mix well. Pour evenly into prepared cake pans.

3. Bake 45 to 50 minutes or until toothpick inserted into centers comes out clean. Poke holes in warm cakes with wooden skewer. Combine reserved canned pineapple juice with enough pineapple juice to equal 2 cups. Pour 1 cup over each cake. Allow cakes to soak up juice and cool in pans.

4. Prepare Cream Cheese Frosting.

5. Invert one cake layer onto serving plate; frost top of cake. Place second cake layer on top of first cake layer. Frost top and sides of cake. Decorate cake by using icing spreader to make peaks with frosting. Sprinkle remaining 1 tablespoon cinnamon over frosting. Store cake in refrigerator.

Makes 10 to 12 servings

continued on page 110

Moist and Tender Carrot Cake, continued

Cream Cheese Frosting

2 cups butter, softened
1 package (8 ounces) cream cheese, softened
2 tablespoons vanilla
2 cups powdered sugar
  Whipping cream

Beat butter, cream cheese and vanilla in large bowl with electric mixer until light and fluffy. Add powdered sugar until completely combined. If frosting is too thick, thin it out with whipping cream, 1 tablespoon at a time.

Ginger-Peachy Crisp
Marilyn Pocius ❧ *Oak Park, IL*

5 cups sliced peaches
¼ to ½ cup granulated sugar
¾ cup uncooked old-fashioned oats
¾ cup brown sugar
½ cup all-purpose flour
2 tablespoon crystallized ginger, finely chopped
¼ teaspoon nutmeg
¼ cup butter, cut into chunks

1. Preheat oven to 350°F. Grease 8×8-inch baking dish; set aside.

2. Combine peach slices and ¼ cup granulated sugar in medium bowl. Add more sugar if peaches are not sweet enough.

3. Combine oats, brown sugar, flour, ginger and nutmeg in medium bowl. Cut butter into mixture using pastry blender or two knives until coarse crumbs form. Pour peach mixture into prepared pan. Sprinkle oat mixture over peaches.

4. Bake 20 to 30 minutes or until topping is crispy and golden brown.

Makes 6 to 8 servings

Blueberry Crumb Cake
Constance McMorris 🍓 Newberry, SC

2 cups all-purpose flour
⅔ cup sugar
3 teaspoons baking powder
1 teaspoon salt
½ teaspoon baking soda
1 cup milk
½ cup butter or margarine, melted
2 eggs
2 tablespoons lemon juice
2 cups fresh or thawed frozen blueberries
Crumb Topping (recipe follows)

1. Preheat oven to 375°F. Grease 13×9-inch baking dish. Set aside.

2. Sift four, sugar, baking powder, salt and baking soda into large bowl.

3. Combine milk, butter, eggs and lemon juice in medium bowl. Pour into flour mixture. Stir until blended.

4. Pour mixture into prepared dish. Sprinkle blueberries evenly over batter. Prepare Crumb Topping.

5. Sprinkle cake with Crumb Topping and bake 40 to 45 minutes. Serve warm.
Makes 6 to 8 servings

Crumb Topping: Combine 1 cup chopped walnuts or pecans, ⅔ cup sugar, ½ cup all-purpose flour, 4 tablespoons softened butter or margarine and ½ teaspoon cinnamon in large bowl.

Ginger Spice Roll

3 eggs, separated
½ cup light molasses
½ cup butter, softened
¼ cup sugar
1 cup all-purpose flour
¾ teaspoon baking soda
½ teaspoon ginger
½ teaspoon cinnamon
½ teaspoon cloves
¼ teaspoon nutmeg
  Spiced Filling (recipe follows)
  Vanilla ice cream (optional)

1. Preheat oven to 375°F. Grease 15×10×1-inch jelly-roll pan. Line pan with parchment paper and grease; dust pan with flour.

2. Beat egg yolks in large bowl with electric mixer at high until mixture turns thick and yellow, about 3 to 4 minutes. Add molasses and butter; beat 1 minute.

3. Beat egg whites in small bowl until foamy. Add sugar, beating until soft peaks form. Fold into egg yolk mixture.

4. Sift flour, baking soda, ginger, cinnamon, cloves and nutmeg into small bowl. Fold into egg mixture; mix well, scraping sides and bottom of bowl.

5. Pour batter into prepared pan. Bake 10 to 12 minutes or until cake is golden and edges begin to pull away from sides of pan. Dust clean linen towel with powdered sugar. Remove pan from oven and invert cake onto sugared towel. Peel off parchment paper, and gently roll cake with towel, starting from short side. Cool cake completely.

6. Prepare Spiced Filling.

7. Unroll cake, spread with Spiced Filling, reroll and sprinkle with more powdered sugar. Serve with vanilla ice cream, if desired.

Makes 8 to 10 servings

Spiced Filling

1 package (8 ounces) cream cheese, softened
¼ cup butter
1 cup powdered sugar
½ teaspoon vanilla
¼ teaspoon ginger
¼ teaspoon cinnamon

Beat cream cheese and butter in medium bowl. Stir in powdered sugar, vanilla and spices. Blend until smooth.

Mom's Bread Pudding

Debra Schoeller ❧ *Noblesville, IN*

5 cups day old cubed bread
2½ cups warm milk
¾ cups sugar, divided
1½ teaspoons cinnamon, divided
1 teaspoon vanilla
¾ teaspoon nutmeg
2 eggs, beaten

Preheat oven to 350°F. Combine bread cubes and milk in large bowl. Pour into 9×9-inch baking pan. Combine ½ cup sugar, 1 teaspoon cinnamon, vanilla and nutmeg in medium bowl. Beat eggs in medium bowl with electric mixer 1 minute. Add to sugar mixture. Pour sugar mixture over bread cubes; stir quickly. Combine remaining ¼ cup sugar and remaining ½ teaspoon cinnamon in small bowl. Sprinkle over bread cubes. Bake 50 to 60 minutes or until center is set. *Makes 10 servings*

Hawaiian Fruit and Nut Quick Bread

Dorothy J. Kapahua ❧ Ft. Myers, FL

2 cups all-purpose flour
2 teaspoons baking soda
1 teaspoon cinnamon
1 tablespoon orange-flavored instant drink powder
¾ cup granulated sugar
¾ cup light brown sugar
¾ cup chopped macadamia nuts
½ cup shredded coconut
¾ cup canola oil
2 teaspoons rum extract
2 eggs
2 cups chopped fresh mango

1. Preheat oven to 350°F. Lightly grease 9×3-inch loaf pan. Set aside.

2. Sift flour with baking soda, cinnamon and drink powder into medium bowl. Stir in sugars, macadamia nuts and coconut. Combine canola oil, rum extract and eggs in separate medium bowl. Add to dry mixture and stir to mix well. Stir in mango.

3. Spoon ingredients into prepared pan. Bake 60 to 70 minutes or until bread is light golden brown in color and pulls away from sides of pan. Cool in pan 10 minutes. Remove to wire rack and cool completely.   *Makes 1 loaf*

Helpful Hint

Mangoes should be firm but not hard. The flesh should yield slightly to pressure. Somewhat hard ones will ripen at home although rock-hard mangoes most likely will rot before they ripen. The skin should be taut, smooth and free of black spots and shriveled ends. Black speckling on the skin is perfectly acceptable. A sweet, fruity aroma around the stem end is indicative of a good specimen.

*Hawaiian Fruit and Nut
Quick Bread*

Dorothy J. Kapahua

Warm Apple & Blueberry Crisp

Sheri Culler ❧ Lucas, Ohio

6 medium apples, peeled, cored and cut into cubes
2 cups thawed frozen blueberries
½ cup brown sugar, divided
¼ cup orange juice
½ cup buttermilk baking mix
½ cup uncooked old-fashioned oats
¼ cup butter, cut into bits
¼ teaspoon cinnamon
¼ teaspoon ginger

1. Preheat oven to 375°F. Spray 9-inch square or round baking pan with nonstick cooking spray. Set aside.

2. Combine apples, blueberries, ¼ cup brown sugar and orange juice in medium bowl. Transfer to prepared pan.

3. Combine baking mix, oats, remaining ¼ cup brown sugar, butter, cinnamon and ginger in small bowl. Mix until coarse crumbs form. Sprinkle mixture evenly over fruit. Bake 45 minutes or until apples are tender.

Makes 6 servings

Orange Bread

Sandra Marie Swift ❧ Pensacola, FL

1 cup honey
2 tablespoons shortening
1 orange
1 egg, beaten
2⅔ cups all-purpose flour
2½ teaspoons baking powder
½ teaspoon salt
½ teaspoon baking soda
½ cup orange juice
¾ cup sliced blanched almonds

Preheat oven to 325°F. Grease 9×2-inch loaf pan. Set aside. Beat honey and shortening in large bowl with electric mixer. Grate orange rind to equal 1½ tablespoons. Peel, seed and chop remaining orange; set aside. Add egg and orange rind to honey mixture. Sift flour, baking powder, salt and baking soda into medium bowl. Add to honey mixture alternately with orange juice. Stir in orange and almonds. Pour batter into prepared pan. Bake 70 minutes or until toothpick inserted into center comes out clean.   *Makes 10 to 12 servings*

Rhubarb Tart

Marilyn Pocius ❧ Oak Park, IL

1 unbaked 9-inch pie crust
4 cups rhubarb, cut into ½-inch pieces
1¼ cups sugar
¼ cup all-purpose flour
2 tablespoons butter, cut into chunks
¼ cup uncooked old-fashioned oats

Preheat oven to 450°F. Line 9-inch pie plate with pie crust; set aside. Combine rhubarb, sugar and flour in medium bowl. Pour into pie crust. Top with chunks of butter. Sprinkle oats over rhubarb. Bake 10 minutes. *Reduce oven temperature to 350°F.* Bake 40 minutes more or until bubbly.

Makes 8 servings

Leftover Coffee Dessert
Marliss Dykes ❧ Hazlehurst, GA

6½ cups very strong coffee
2 cinnamon sticks
4 whole cloves
3 envelopes unflavored gelatin
½ cup cold water
1 cup brown sugar
¾ cup toasted chopped Brazil nuts
1 teaspoon minced crystallized ginger
Whipped topping (optional)

Combine coffee, cinnamon sticks and cloves in medium saucepan. Heat over low heat 10 minutes. Remove cinnamon sticks and cloves. Combine gelatin and cold water in medium bowl. Add gelatin and brown sugar to coffee. Stir until dissolved. Pour into 13×9-inch baking pan. Chill 2 hours or until mixture begins to set. Fold in nuts and ginger. Chill 2 more hours or until firm. Cut into 1-inch squares and place in individual bowls with dollops of whipped topping, if desired.   *Makes 4 servings*

Marliss says:

*Add a teaspoon of Irish Cream flavoring to the whipped cream
for a special treat.*

Mother's Sugarless Cake

Margaret Pache ❧ Mesa, AZ

2 cups dried cranberries
2 cups orange juice
1 cup unsweetened applesauce
¾ cup oil
2 eggs, beaten
2 tablespoons liquid sweetener
2 cups all purpose flour
1 teaspoon baking soda
1 teaspoon cinnamon
1 teaspoon lemon extract
Applesauce, for garnish
Whipped cream, for garnish

Preheat oven to 350°F. Spray 8-inch baking pan with nonstick cooking spray. Set aside. Combine cranberries and orange juice in medium saucepan. Heat over medium heat 5 to 8 minutes. Remove from heat. Add applesauce, oil, eggs and sweetener. Mix well.

Combine flour, baking soda and cinnamon in medium bowl. Add to cranberry mixture. Add lemon extract. Pour into prepared pan. Bake 20 to 25 minutes. Cut into small squares. Garnish with applesauce and whipped cream.

Makes 12 to 16 servings

Aunt Lucille's Chocolate Pound Cake

Rebecca J. Lacy   Claremore, OK

3 cups all-purpose flour
4 to 5 tablespoons cocoa powder
3 teaspoons baking powder
¼ teaspoon salt
½ cup margarine or butter
½ cup shortening
3 cups sugar
4 eggs
1 cup sweetened condensed milk
1 teaspoon vanilla
Chocolate Frosting (recipe follows)

Preheat oven to 350°F. Grease 10-inch Bundt pan. Set aside. Sift flour, cocoa, baking powder and salt into large bowl. Beat margarine and shortening in another large bowl. Gradually add sugar. Add eggs, one at a time, beating well after each addition. Gradually add flour mixture and milk. Add vanilla; mix well. Pour into prepared pan. Bake 1 hour 15 minutes or until toothpick inserted near center comes out clean. Cool cake on wire rack. Prepare Chocolate Frosting. Invert cake onto serving plate. Frost top and sides of cake.

Makes 12 servings

Chocolate Frosting

2 squares (1 ounce each) unsweetened chocolate, chopped
¾ cup sweetened condensed milk
2 cups sugar
3 to 4 tablespoons butter or margarine
¼ teaspoon salt
1 teaspoon vanilla

Combine chocolate and milk in medium saucepan. Cook over low heat, stirring constantly, until almost thickened. Add sugar; bring to a boil. Boil 9 to 10 minutes, stirring frequently. Add butter and salt; remove from heat. Cool 20 minutes. Add vanilla and beat until spreadable.

*Aunt Lucille's
Chocolate Pound Cake*

Date Loaf

Harriet E. Smith ❧ Ocala, FL

1 package (8 ounces) pitted dates
2 cups miniature marshmallows
1 cup milk
2 cups graham cracker crumbs, divided
1 cup pecans (optional)
  Whipped topping (optional)

Chop dates; set aside. Combine marshmallows and milk in medium bowl. Allow marshmallows to absorb some of the milk. Add dates, 1½ cups graham cracker crumbs and pecans, if desired, to marshmallow mixture; mix well. (Mixture will be moist.)

Sprinkle ¼ cup graham cracker crumbs on waxed paper. Place date mixture on waxed paper and form into loaf shape. Sprinkle remaining ¼ cup graham cracker crumbs over top and sides of loaf. Wrap in aluminum foil and refrigerate until firm. Slice and serve with whipped topping, if desired.

Makes 8 to 10 servings

French Vanilla Bread Pudding

Margaret D. Volk ❧ LeRoy, IL

2 cups low-fat or regular french vanilla-flavored coffee creamer
1 cup sugar
½ cup butter
5 large eggs *or* 1¼ cups cholesterol-free egg substitute
1 pound day old unfrosted cinnamon rolls, cut into 1-inch cubes
1 cup raisins
½ cup chopped pecans (optional)
1 can (21 ounces) apple or cherry pie filling
  Whipped Topping

Preheat oven to 350°F. Grease 13×9-inch pan. Set aside.

Combine coffee creamer, sugar and butter in medium saucepan. Heat over medium heat until butter is melted, stirring occasionally. Cool; whisk in eggs. Place cinnamon roll cubes and raisins in prepared pan. Pour egg mixture over bread cubes. Allow egg mixture to soak into cinnamon roll cubes, stirring occasionally. Sprinkle pecans, if desired, over cinnamon roll mixture. Bake 30 minutes or until set. Cool. Top with pie filling and whipped topping.

Makes 12 servings

Lemon Layered Dessert
Heather Samples ❧ Cumming, GA

    1 cup all-purpose flour
    ½ cup nuts
    ½ cup butter
    1 container (12 ounces) frozen whipped topping, thawed, divided
    1 cup powdered sugar
    1 package (8 ounces) cream cheese, softened
    2 packages (4-serving size) lemon-flavored instant pudding mix
    2½ cups milk

Preheat oven to 350°F. Combine flour and nuts in medium bowl. Mix in butter with pastry blender or two knives until mixture resembles coarse crumbs. Press into bottom of 13×9-inch baking pan. Bake 10 minutes. Cool completely.

Beat 2 cups whipped topping and powdered sugar in medium bowl with electric mixer until smooth. Spread over crust.

Beat pudding mix and milk in medium bowl until thick. Spread over cream cheese layer. Spread remaining whipped topping over lemon mixture. Refrigerate until ready to serve.

Makes 12 to 16 servings

Daddy's Favorite Pineapple Pudding

Mary G. Taylor ❧ Murfreesboro, TN

1¾ cups sugar, divided
½ cup flour
2½ cups milk
¼ cup margarine
3 eggs, separated
1 teaspoon vanilla
1 can (20 ounces) chunk pineapple, drained, juice reserved
½ package (6 ounces) vanilla wafers

Preheat oven to 375°F.

Combine 1½ cups sugar and flour in medium saucepan. Add milk, margarine, egg yolks and vanilla. Bring to a boil, stirring constantly. Add reserved pineapple juice. Bring to a boil. Remove from heat and add pineapple chunks.

Line 13×9-inch baking dish with vanilla wafers. Pour pineapple mixture over wafers.

Beat egg whites in medium bowl until stiff peaks form. Add remaining ¼ cup sugar and beat thoroughly. Spread over pudding.

Bake 8 to 10 minutes or until top is lightly browned.   *Makes 12 servings*

Double Vanilla Cookie Parfait

William P. Hand ❧ Ewing Twp. Trenton, NJ

1 package (4-serving size) sugar-free French vanilla-flavored instant
    pudding mix
1¾ cups vanilla soy milk
6 sugar-free chocolate chip cookies, crushed

1. Prepare pudding according to package directions substituting soy milk for milk.

2. Place ¼ cup pudding into 4 dessert bowls. Sprinkle 1¼ crushed cookies over pudding in each bowl. Top with remaining pudding. Cover and chill.

Makes 4 (½ cup) servings

Cinnamon Bake

Daniel Javier ❧ Torrance, CA

⅔ cup all-purpose flour
2⅓ cups dark brown sugar
1½ cups granulated sugar
¼ cup cinnamon
¼ cup unsweetened cocoa powder
¼ cup cornstarch
⅛ cup baking powder
⅓ cup water
⅓ cup vegetable oil
1 egg
2 tablespoon butter

Preheat oven to 400°F. Grease 11×7-inch baking dish. Set aside.

Combine flour, sugars, cinnamon, cocoa powder, cornstarch and baking powder in large bowl. Add water, oil, egg and butter. Mix well. Pour batter into prepared pan.

Bake 30 to 35 minutes or until toothpick inserted into center comes out clean. Cool 20 minutes. Serve as desired. *Makes 8 to 10 servings*

No Bake Treats

Vanilla Ice Cream Loaf

Helen Fan ❧ Cupertino, CA

¼ cup powdered sugar
1 to 2 teaspoons water
1½ quarts vanilla ice cream, softened
1 package (3 ounces) ladyfingers
Raspberry or strawberry sauce, for garnish
Fresh or thawed frozen raspberries or strawberries (optional)

Line 9×5-inch loaf pan with plastic wrap leaving 2½ inch overhangs. Combine powdered sugar and water in small bowl; mix until mixture resembles paste. Split ladyfingers. Spread a small amount of powdered sugar mixture on outside bottom of 1 ladyfinger and anchor it upright against side of pan. Repeat with remaining ladyfingers, making border around pan. Beat ice cream in large bowl with electric mixer until smooth. Spread into pan, pressing against ladyfingers. Cover and freeze 6 hours. Place in refrigerator 20 minutes before serving. To serve, drizzle 1 tablespoon sauce on individual serving plates. Cut Vanilla Ice Cream Loaf into slices. Place on plate over sauce. Drizzle another 1 tablespoon sauce over top. Top with raspberries, if desired.

Makes 8 servings

Banana Split Cake

Tami Crosby ❧ Glendale, AZ

1¼ cups sugar, divided
½ cup margarine, softened
1 package graham crackers (about 20)
2 packages (8 ounces each) cream cheese
4 to 5 bananas
1 can (20 ounces) crushed pineapple, drained
1 container (12 ounces) frozen whipped topping, thawed
¼ cup chopped pecans or walnuts

Beat ¼ cup sugar and margarine in medium bowl with electric mixer at medium speed until creamed. Finely crush graham crackers in resealable plastic food storage bag with rolling pin. Add to margarine mixture. Press into bottom of well greased 13×9-inch baking dish.

Beat cream cheese and remaining 1 cup sugar until creamy. Spread over cracker crust. Slice bananas and layer over cream cheese mixture. Spread pineapple over bananas. Spread whipped topping over pineapple. Sprinkle with pecans. Chill 4 to 6 hours.   *Makes 8 servings*

Angel Food Dream Cake

Marguerite M. Campbell ❧ *Pittsburgh, PA*

1 homemade or store-bought round angel food cake
2 packages (4-serving size each) vanilla-flavored instant pudding mix
2 cups milk
1 container (8 ounces) frozen whipped topping, thawed
2 cans (21 ounces each) blueberry pie filling

Cut angel food cake into 1-inch cubes. Place in bottom of 11×9-inch pan. Combine pudding mixes and milk in large bowl. Fold in whipped topping. Spread over cake cubes. Top with pie filling. Chill overnight.

Makes 8 to 10 servings

Marguerite says:

Substitute your favorite flavor pie filling for the blueberry pie filling.

Eclaire Dessert

Vikki Fry ❧ *Monterey, TN*

2 packages (4-serving size each) vanilla-flavored instant pudding mix
3 cups milk
1 container (8 ounces) frozen whipped topping, thawed
1 box (32 ounces) graham crackers
1 container (16 ounces) chocolate frosting

Beat pudding and milk in large bowl with electric mixer. Fold in whipped topping. Place 1 layer graham crackers in 13×9-inch cake pan. Top with 1 layer pudding mixture. Repeat layers using remaining graham crackers and pudding mixture ending with layer of graham crackers. Spread frosting over graham crackers. Refrigerate 4 hours or overnight.

Makes 12 servings

Peanut Butter Fudge

Brenda Hebron ❧ West Lafayette, OH

1½ cups granulated sugar
1½ cups packed brown sugar
½ cup milk
1 tablespoon unsweetened cocoa powder
1 cup creamy or chunky peanut butter
½ cup butter or margarine
1 teaspoon vanilla

Combine sugars, milk and cocoa in large saucepan. Cook over medium heat, stirring constantly, until mixture reaches 238°F (soft ball stage) on candy thermometer.

Remove from heat; add peanut butter, butter and vanilla. Stir until melted. Pour into greased 13×9-inch pan (or, use 9×9-inch pan for thicker fudge). Cool completely. Cut into 1-inch squares.   *Makes about 1¼ pounds fudge*

Helpful Hint

For easy clean-up line pan with greased foil. Simply lift fudge out of pan and cut into pieces.

Cookies and Cream Layered Dessert

Phyllis Tatro ❧ Springfield, MA

1 cup cold milk

1 package (4-serving size) white chocolate-flavored instant pudding
mix

1 package chocolate creme-filled sandwich cookies

¼ cup butter, melted

2 packages (8 ounces each) cream cheese, softened

2 cups powdered sugar

1 container (8 ounces) frozen whipped topping, thawed

1 teaspoon vanilla

1 pint whipping cream

Combine milk and pudding mix in medium bowl. Set aside.

Finely crush cookies in resealable plastic food storage bag with rolling pin or
in blender. Combine 2 cups crushed cookies and butter in small bowl. Place
on bottom of 2-quart trifle dish. Reserve remaining crushed cookies.

Beat cream cheese and powdered sugar in large bowl with electric mixer at
medium speed. Fold in pudding mixture, whipped topping and vanilla.

Beat whipping cream in small bowl with electric mixer until soft peaks form.
Fold into cream cheese mixture.

Spread layer of cream cheese mixture over cookie crust. Sprinkle 1 layer of
cookie crumbs over cream cheese layer. Repeat layers using remaining cream
cheese mixture and cookie crumbs until top of dish is reached. Garnish with
remaining cookie crumbs. Refrigerate until ready to serve.

Makes 12 servings

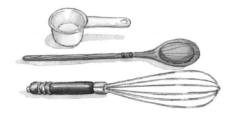

Strawberry Delight Salad

Diane Graham ❧ Norwalk, IA

1 package (8 ounces) cream cheese, softened
1 package (10 ounces) frozen strawberries, thawed, accumulated juice
    reserved
1 cup canned pears, drained
1 container (8 ounces) frozen whipped topping, thawed
½ cup chopped walnuts
    Fresh strawberries, for garnish (optional)

Beat cream cheese and reserved strawberry juice in cold large bowl with electric mixer until smooth. Add remaining ingredients; mix well. Pour into decorative bowl. Cover and chill 1 hour or overnight. Garnish with fresh strawberries, if desired.

Makes 8 servings

Apricot Fluff Shortcakes

Mavis Gannello ❧ Oak Park, IL

2 cups frozen whipped topping, thawed
4 tablespoons apricot preserves
5 shortcake shells (1 ounce each)
1 cup fresh blueberries
1 tablespoon sugar

Beat whipped topping and apricot preserves in large bowl with electric mixer until well blended. Place a dollop on each shortcake shell.

Combine blueberries and sugar in small bowl. Place each shortcake on individual serving plates. Sprinkle blueberries over whipped topping.

Makes 5 servings

Lemon Chiffon

Vicki Morang ❧ Eastport, ME

2 packages (4-serving size each) lemon-flavored gelatin
2 packages (4-serving size each) vanilla-flavored instant pudding mix
3 cups boiling water
1 container (8 ounces) frozen whipped topping, thawed

1. Combine gelatin and pudding mix into 5-quart serving bowl. Add boiling water, whisking constantly to dissolve completely. Refrigerate until mixture cools and thickens slightly, about 1 hour.

2. Stir in whipped topping and chill until mixture sets, at least 1 hour.

Makes 12 servings

❧ Vickie says: ❧

*This can be made with combinations of other flavors of gelatin and pudding.
Try sugar-free gelatin and pudding for a lower calorie treat.*

Strawberry Angel Food Dessert

Mardel Barnette ❧ Comstock, WI

3 packages (4-serving size each) strawberry-flavored gelatin
4 cups boiling water
2 packages (16 ounces each) frozen strawberries
1 homemade or store-bought angel food cake
½ container (4 ounces) frozen whipped topping, thawed

Combine gelatin and water in large bowl. Stir until gelatin is dissolved. Add strawberries; stir until strawberries are thawed. Let stand until thickened. Tear angel food cake into bite-sized pieces. Fold into strawberry mixture. Fold in whipped topping. Spread cake mixture in to 15×11-inch pan. Refrigerate until ready to serve. *Makes 12 to 15 servings*

Crunch Peanut Butter Chocolate Fudge

Emily Levy ❧ Philadelphia, PA

½ cup light corn syrup
¼ cup packed brown sugar
⅛ teaspoon salt
1 cup peanut butter
1 cup crisp rice cereal
1 cup cornflakes
1 cup semi-sweet chocolate chips
1 teaspoon vanilla
  Powdered sugar

Combine corn syrup, brown sugar and salt in 2-quart saucepan. Bring to a boil, stirring occasionally. Add peanut butter; remove from heat. Stir in cereals, chocolate chips and vanilla. Press into 9×9×2-inch pan. Chill 1 hour or overnight. Cut into 1-inch squares and sprinkle with powdered sugar.

Makes about 1 pound fudge

Strawberry Salad

Carol Hale ❧ Paris, OH

2 packages (4-serving size each) strawberry-flavored gelatin
1 cup boiling water
2 packages (10 ounces each) frozen strawberries, thawed
1 can (20 ounces) crushed pineapple, drained
1 container (2 cups) sour cream

Combine gelatin and water in large bowl; stir until dissolved. Add strawberries and pineapple; mix well. Pour half of gelatin mixture into 13×9-inch pan. Refrigerate until set. Spread sour cream over gelatin in pan. Pour remaining gelatin mixture over sour cream. Refrigerate until ready to serve.

Makes 12 to 14 servings

Frozen Mocha Dessert

Nancy Anderson ❧ Yarmouth Port, MA

1 cup chocolate cookie crumbs (about 18 chocolate wafer cookies)
3 tablespoons margarine or butter, melted
¼ cup instant coffee granules
2 tablespoons hot water
3 packages (3 ounces each) reduced-fat cream cheese, softened
1 can (14 ounces) fat-free sweetened condensed milk
¾ cup reduced-calorie chocolate syrup
2 containers (8 ounces each) frozen whipped topping, thawed

1. Combine cookie crumbs and margarine in medium bowl Press into 10-inch springform pan. Chill.

2. Dissolve instant coffee in hot water in small bowl. Beat cream cheese in medium bowl with electric mixer until fluffy. Beat in coffee mixture, condensed milk and chocolate syrup. Carefully fold in whipped topping until well blended.

3. Pour filling over cookie crust; tap gently on counter to remove air bubbles. Cover with plastic wrap and place in freezer at least 6 hours. Garnish as desired.   *Makes 12 servings*

Abuelita Arsenia's Favorite Dessert

Alma Meyers ❧ Victorville, CA

2 packages (4-serving size each) vanilla-flavored instant pudding mix, plus ingredients to prepare

3 packages (24 cookies each) ladyfingers

2 packages (4-serving size each) chocolate-flavored instant pudding mix, plus ingredients to prepare

2 packages (4-serving size each) butterscotch-flavored instant pudding mix, plus ingredients to prepare

1 container (8 ounces) sour cream

2 tablespoons sugar or more to taste

1 can (16 ounces) prepared chocolate fudge frosting

1. Prepare vanilla pudding as directed on package. Dip 1 package of ladyfingers, one at a time, into pudding. Arrange in single layer in 13×9-inch pan. If extra pudding remains, spread over ladyfingers. Repeat with chocolate and butterscotch pudding mixes and remaining 2 packages of ladyfingers.

2. Beat sour cream and sugar in medium bowl with electric mixer, adding additional sugar to taste. Spread evenly over butterscotch pudding layer. Cover and refrigerate 1 hour.

3. Remove from refrigerator and top with frosting. Cover and refrigerate overnight or until ready to serve. *Makes 12 to 14 servings*

Cheesecake Dessert

Tammy Reigle 🍓 Moncks Corner, SC

3 cups milk
2 packages (4-serving size each) cheesecake-flavored instant pudding
   mix
1 cup powdered sugar
2 containers (8 ounces each) frozen whipped topping, thawed
1 package (32 ounces) graham crackers
1 can (21 ounces) cherry pie filling

Combine milk, pudding mix, powdered sugar and 1 container whipped topping in large bowl; mix well. Set aside. Grease 11×8-inch pan. Line pan with graham crackers. Spread half of pudding mixture over crackers and top with another layer of graham crackers. Repeat layers with remaining pudding mixture and graham crackers. Spread remaining container of whipped topping over last layer of graham crackers. Top with pie filling. Refrigerate 4 hours or overnight. *Makes 10 servings*

Excellent Mint Wafers

Helen Fan 🍓 Cupertino, CA

3½ to 4 cups powdered sugar
⅔ cup sweetened condensed milk
   Food coloring, any color
½ teaspoon peppermint, spearmint or wintergreen extract

Line baking sheet with waxed paper. Combine 3½ cups powdered sugar and condensed milk in large bowl. Add food coloring, a few drops at a time, until desired color is obtained. Knead in extract and enough powdered sugar until smooth creamy texture is reached. Shape mixture into 1-inch balls. Place about 1 inch apart on baking sheet. Flatten each ball with fork to about ¼-inch thickness. Let stand, uncovered, at room temperature about 1 hour or until firm. *Makes about 1 pound candy*

Mom's Heavenly Berry Cake

Loralee K. Pillsbury ❧ Fort Carson, CO

1 package (4-serving size) sugar-free strawberry- or raspberry-flavored gelatin, plus ingredients to prepare

1 homemade or store-bought angel food cake

1 package (4-serving size) vanilla-flavored instant pudding mix, plus ingredients to prepare

1 quart strawberries, stemmed and halved

¼ cup slivered almonds

Prepare gelatin mix according to package directions. Refrigerate one hour.

Meanwhile, crumble angel food cake in to 13×9-inch baking dish. Prepare pudding according to package directions.

Pour gelatin mixture over cake. Place 1 layer of strawberries over cake. Spread pudding over strawberries. Sprinkle almonds over pudding layer. Garnish with remaining strawberries. Refrigerate at least 1 hour or until ready to serve.

Makes 12 servings

❧ Loralee says: ❧

You can substitute any kind of berry, nut or pudding flavor in this recipe.

Tammy's Triple Banana Treat

Tammy Reigle ❧ Moncks Corner, SC

1 box (32 ounces) graham crackers
3 cups milk
2 containers (8 ounces each) frozen whipped topping, thawed
1 cup powdered sugar
2 packages (4-serving size each) banana-flavored instant pudding mix
6 bananas
½ cup walnuts

1. Lightly grease 11×8-inch pan. Line pan with layer of graham crackers. Set aside.

2. Combine milk, 1 container whipped topping, powdered sugar and pudding mix in large bowl.

3. Pour half of pudding mixture over crackers. Slice 2 bananas. Place slices over pudding. Repeat layers using remaining graham crackers, remaining pudding mixture and 2 bananas. Place 1 layer graham crackers over banana layer. Spread remaining container whipped topping over graham crackers.

4. Slice remaining 2 bananas and place on top of whipped topping. Sprinkle with walnuts.

5. Refrigerate at least 4 hours or overnight.   *Makes 10 to 12 servings*

Quick Berry Trifle

Julie Bottrell ❧ Canyon Lake, CA

2 cups sliced strawberries
1 cup raspberries or blackberries
1 cup blueberries
¼ cup sugar
1 pound cake (about 12 ounces), cut into ½-inch-thick slices
1 container (28 ounces) prepared vanilla pudding
1 can (7 ounces) whipped topping

1. Combine berries and sugar in a medium bowl, stirring gently to combine.

2. Place single layer of cake slices in bottom of deep serving bowl. Top with ⅓ of pudding, then ⅓ of berries. Repeat layers twice, using remaining ingredients. Cover tightly with plastic wrap and refrigerate for at least 1 hour or until ready to serve.

3. Just before serving, remove from refrigerator. Remove plastic wrap; top with whipped topping. Serve as desired. *Makes 12 servings*

Frozen Chocolate Cookie Cake

Gina Cramer 🍂 *Noah Branch, MI*

> 30 chocolate creme-filled sandwich cookies
> ¾ cup butter, divided
> ½ gallon vanilla ice cream, softened
> 1 can (16 ounces) chocolate syrup
> 1 can (14 ounces) sweetened condensed milk
> 1 container (8 ounces) frozen whipped topping, thawed
> Chopped nuts (optional)

1. Finely crush cookies in resealable plastic food storage bag with rolling pin or in blender. Sprinkle in bottom of 13×9-inch pan. Melt ¼ cup butter in small saucepan. Pour over cookies in pan. Freeze 15 minutes.

2. Spread ice cream over crust. Freeze 15 minutes more.

3. Combine chocolate syrup, condensed milk and remaining ½ cup butter in medium saucepan. Bring to a boil; cool completely.

4. Pour chocolate syrup mixture over ice cream. Spread whipped topping over chocolate syrup mixture. Sprinkle with chopped nuts, if desired. Freeze until ready to serve. *Makes 10 to 12 servings*

Pam's Peanut Butter Balls

Pamela R. Walker 🍂 *Houston, TX*

> ¾ cup creamy or chunky peanut butter
> ¾ cup corn syrup
> ½ cup sugar
> 8½ cups cornflakes
> ½ teaspoon vanilla

Combine peanut butter, corn syrup and sugar in large saucepan. Melt over low heat, stirring constantly. Stir in corn flakes and vanilla. Spread mixture immediately onto baking sheet. Cool 5 minutes. Form mixture into 1-inch balls. Return to baking sheet. Refrigerate 10 minutes or until ready to serve. *Makes 24 balls*

Strawberry Dessert

Tina M. Cartee ❧ Mentor on the Lake, OH

1 cup margarine, softened and divided
2 cups graham cracker crumbs
1 package (16 ounces) powdered sugar
2 eggs
1 can (8 ounces) crushed pineapple, well-drained
2 to 3 containers frozen strawberries with juice, thawed
1 container (12 ounces) frozen whipped topping, thawed

1. Melt ½ cup margarine in small saucepan over medium heat. Combine cracker crumbs and margarine in medium bowl. Press into bottom of 13×9-inch baking dish.

2. Combine remaining ½ cup margarine and powdered sugar in medium bowl. Beat in eggs with electric mixer until fluffy. Pour over cracker crust.

3. Spread pineapple over powdered sugar mixture. Pour strawberries with juice over pineapple. Spread whipped topping over strawberries.

4. Chill at least 4 hours or overnight before serving.

Makes 10 to 12 servings

Impressive Sweets

Chocolate Truffle Torte

Marie McConnell ❧ Las Cruces, NM

1½ cups milk
1 package (12 ounces) semi-sweet chocolate chips
6 squares (1 ounce each) unsweetened baking chocolate, chopped
1 cup brown sugar
1 container (8 ounces) pasteurized cholesterol-free egg substitute
2 teaspoons vanilla

1. Heat milk in medium saucepan over medium-low heat just until bubbles appear around edge of saucepan.

2. Combine chocolate chips, chopped chocolate and brown sugar in blender. Pour hot milk into blender and carefully blend until smooth. With blender still running, add egg substitute and vanilla.

3. Pour chocolate mixture into 9-inch springform pan. Cover and chill at least 6 hours or overnight.   *Makes 12 to 16 servings*

❧ Marie says: ❧

Serve with whipped cream and puréed raspberries or strawberries.

Marie McConnell

Citrus Rum Cake

Crystal French ❦ Hinsdale, IL

3 cups all-purpose flour
2 cups sugar
2 teaspoons baking powder
½ teaspoon salt
1 cup orange juice
½ cup butter, melted
3 eggs
½ cup pecans, chopped
½ cup golden rum, divided

1. Preheat oven to 350°F. Grease 10-inch Bundt pan. Set aside.

2. Combine flour, sugar, baking powder and salt in medium bowl. Blend in orange juice, butter and eggs with electric mixer.

3. Stir in pecans by hand, scraping down sides and bottom of bowl. Stir in ¼ cup rum. Pour batter into prepared pan.

4. Bake 50 to 60 minutes or until toothpick inserted near center comes out clean. Remove from oven and cool. Drizzle with remaining ¼ cup rum, and invert onto serving plate. *Makes 12 servings*

Lemon Chiffon Cake

Helen Fan 🌿 Cupertino, CA

2 cups all-purpose flour
1½ cups sugar
3 teaspoons baking powder
1 teaspoon salt
¾ cup cold water
½ cup vegetable oil
2 teaspoons vanilla
2 teaspoons grated lemon peel
7 egg yolks
1 cup egg whites (about 8)
½ teaspoon cream of tartar
Powdered sugar

1. Preheat oven to 325°F.

2. Combine flour, sugar, baking powder and salt in large bowl. Beat in water, oil, vanilla, lemon peel and egg yolks with spoon until smooth.

3. Beat egg whites and cream of tartar in medium bowl with electric mixer until stiff peaks form. Fold egg yolk mixture into egg whites until blended.

4. Pour into ungreased 10-inch tube pan. Bake 1¼ hours or until top springs back when lightly touched. Invert pan onto glass bottle or funnel. Let it rest for about 2 hours or until completely cooled. Remove from pan. Sprinkle with powdered sugar. *Makes 12 servings*

Nested Sweet Chocolate Mousse

Catherine Hite 🌿 St. Michaels, MD

2 egg whites
⅛ teaspoon salt
⅛ teaspoon cream of tartar
½ cup sugar
½ cup chopped pecans
1½ teaspoons vanilla, divided
1 package (12 ounces) German sweet chocolate
3 tablespoons water
1 cup whipping cream

1. Preheat oven to 300°F. Grease 8-inch pie plate. Set aside.

2. Beat egg whites, salt and cream of tartar in large bowl with electric mixer until foamy. Add sugar, 2 tablespoons at a time, beating well after each addition. Continue to beat until stiff peaks form. Fold in nuts and ½ teaspoon vanilla.

3. Spoon egg white mixture into prepared pie plate and make a shallow well in the middle. Bake 50 to 55 minutes, or until meringue is solid and crisp but not brown. Cool completely.

4. Place chocolate and water in small saucepan over low heat; stir until melted. Add remaining 1 teaspoon vanilla. Cool completely. Beat whipping cream in medium bowl until soft peaks form. Fold chocolate mixture into cream. Spoon into meringue and chill at least 1 hour before serving.

Makes 8 servings

Caramel Snow Eggs

Helen Fan ❧ Cupertino, CA

Custard Cream

1½ cups milk

1 teaspoon cornstarch

6 egg yolks

⅓ cup sugar

1 teaspoon vanilla

½ cup cold heavy cream

Light Meringues

2 cups water

6 egg whites

¾ cup sugar

Caramel Sauce

½ cup sugar

2 tablespoons water

1. To make Custard Cream, combine milk and cornstarch in medium saucepan. Bring to a boil over medium heat. Set aside. Whisk egg yolks and ⅓ cup sugar in medium bowl until smooth. Pour 2 tablespoons milk mixture into egg yolk mixture. Pour egg yolk mixture into saucepan with remaining milk mixture. Heat over medium heat until it thickens. Remove from heat. Pour cream through strainer into small bowl; add vanilla. Add cream to custard mixture; mix well. Set aside.

2. To make Light Meringues, bring 2 cups water to boil in large saucepan. Reduce to simmer. Beat egg whites in large bowl with electric mixer. Gradually add ¾ cup sugar; beat until stiff peaks form. Using round ice cream scoop, scoop ⅓ cup meringue and smooth off top. Place ball into simmering water. Cook meringue ball 3 minutes per side. Remove to paper towel to drain. Repeat with remaining meringue mixture. Set aside.

3. To prepare Caramel Sauce, combine ½ cup sugar and water in medium saucepan. Boil over medium heat, stirring constantly. Cook until sauce turns light brown. Remove from heat and let thicken.

4. To serve, place 2 tablespoons Custard Cream on individual serving plates. Top each plate with Light Meringue. Drizzle meringues with Caramel Sauce.

Makes 12 servings

Grilled Peaches with Raspberry Sauce

Gina Cramer ❧ North Branch, MI

1 package (10 ounces) frozen raspberries, thawed
1½ teaspoons lemon juice
3 tablespoons brown sugar
1 teaspoons ground cinnamon
3 teaspoons rum (optional)
4 medium peaches, peeled, halved and pitted
2 teaspoons butter
Fresh mint sprigs (optional)

1. Combine raspberries and lemon juice in food processor fitted with metal blade; process until smooth. Chill in refrigerator.

2. Combine brown sugar, cinnamon and rum, if desired, in medium bowl; roll peach halves in mixture. Place peach halves, cut side up, on foil. Dot with butter. Fold foil over peaches and seal loosely. Grill over medium coals for 15 minutes.

3. To serve, spoon 2 tablespoons raspberry sauce over each peach half. Garnish with fresh mint sprig, if desired.   *Makes 4 servings*

Airy Chocolate Cake

Patricia Watkins ❧ Liberty Hill, TX

2 cups all-purpose flour
1 cup butter, melted
½ cup granulated sugar
1 cup chopped pecans
1 package (8 ounces) cream cheese, softened
1 cup powdered sugar
2 containers (8 ounces each) frozen whipped topping, thawed and divided
1 package (4-serving size) vanilla-flavored instant pudding mix
1 package (4-serving size) chocolate-flavored instant pudding mix
3 cups milk

Preheat oven to 350°F. Combine flour, butter and granulated sugar in medium bowl. Reserve 1 tablespoon pecans; set aside. Add remaining pecans to flour mixture. Press into 13×9-inch baking pan. Bake 20 minutes; cool completely.

Beat cream cheese and powdered sugar in medium bowl with electric mixer at medium speed until smooth. Fold in 1 cup whipped topping. Spread over pecan layer.

Combine pudding mixes in large bowl. Add milk; mix well. Spread over cream cheese layer.

Top pudding layer with remaining whipped topping and sprinkle with reserved 1 tablespoon pecans. Refrigerate 4 hours.

Makes 10 to 12 servings.

Chocolate Mousse
Helen Fan ❧ Cupertino, CA

1 package (8 ounces) semi-sweet chocolate chips
6 tablespoons unsalted butter, softened
¼ cup coffee
3 eggs, separated
½ cup whipped cream
¼ cup superfine sugar
    Whipped Cream (optional)

1. Combine chocolate chips, butter and coffee in medium saucepan. Melt over medium heat, stirring constantly.

2. Place egg yolks in medium bowl. Whisk 2 tablespoons chocolate mixture into egg yolks; whisk egg yolk mixture back into chocolate mixture in saucepan. Cook over low heat 2 minutes, whisking contstantly. Remove from heat; cool 3 to 5 minutes.

3. Place whipped cream in medium bowl resting on top of bowl of ice. Beat until soft peaks form. Refrigerate until ready to use.

4. Beat egg whites in medium bowl until soft peaks form. Add sugar, 1 tablespoon at a time. Beat until stiff peaks form and mixture is shiny. Fold into cream mixture. Fold chocolate mixture into cream mixture.

5. Cover and chill 4 hours. Garnish with whipped cream if desired.

Makes 6 servings

Nancy's Tiramisu

Nancy Minor ❧ Phoenix, AZ

6 egg yolks
1¼ cups sugar
1½ cups mascarpone cheese
1¾ cups whipping cream, whipped to soft peaks
1¾ cups cold espresso or strong brewed coffee
3 tablespoons brandy
3 tablespoons grappa
4 packages (3 ounces each) ladyfingers
2 tablespoons powdered, unsweetened cocoa, divided
Whipped cream, for garnish (optional)
Chocolate-covered espresso beans for garnish (optional)

1. Beat egg yolks and sugar in small bowl with electric mixer until fluffy and pale. Place in top of double boiler over boiling water. Reduce heat to low and cook, stirring constantly, 10 minutes. Combine yolk mixture and mascarpone cheese in large bowl and beat with electric mixer at low speed until well blended and fluffy. Fold in whipped cream. Set aside.

2. Combine espresso, brandy and grappa in medium bowl. Dip 24 ladyfingers (use top and bottom) into espresso mixture and arrange side-by-side in single layer in 13×9-inch glass baking dish. Dip ladyfingers in mixture quickly or they will absorb too much liquid and fall apart.

3. Spread ladyfinger layer evenly with half the mascarpone mixture. Sift 1 tablespoon cocoa over marscarpone layer. Repeat with another layer of 24 ladyfingers dipped in espresso mixture. Cover second layer of cookies with remaining mascarpone mixture. Sift remaining 1 tablespoon cocoa over top.

4. Refrigerate at least 4 hours, but preferably overnight, before serving. Cut into slices to serve. Decorate with whipped cream and chocolate-covered espresso beans, if desired. *Makes 12 servings*

Tip: If you can't find marscapone cheese, substitue 1 softened package (8 ounces) cream cheese, ¼ cup sour cream and 2 tablespoons whipping cream. Combine in medium bowl. Beat with electric mixer until light and fluffy.

Glacéed Berries with Pink Meringue

Venta Smith ❧ Newland, NC

1 cup brown sugar
2 tablespoons water
3 tablespoons butter
2 tablespoons grenadine, divided
2 cups strawberries, rinsed and hulled
2 cups blueberries, rinsed
4 egg whites
1 cup granulated sugar

1. Preheat oven to 400°F. Combine brown sugar and water in medium saucepan. Place over high heat and cook, swirling but not stirring, until sugar melts and mixture becomes thick and deep golden brown.

2. Remove sugar mixture from heat and immediately stir in butter and 1 tablespoon grenadine. Add berries and stir until evenly coated; divide berries among 6 oven-safe custard cups. Set aside to cool.

3. When ready to serve, beat egg whites in medium bowl with electric mixer until soft peaks form. Gradually beat in granulated sugar and remaining 1 tablespoon grenadine; beat to stiff peaks. Divide evenly among custard cups, heaping mounds in center of cups and leaving berries visible around edges of cups. Bake 3 or 4 minutes or until meringue is golden brown.

Makes 6 servings

❧ Venta says: ❧

I find it easiest to place all 6 fruit-filled custard cups in a shallow pan or on a baking sheet before topping them with meringue. That way, I can easily place them all into the oven at the same time and I don't have to worry about a cup flipping over or overflowing as it bakes.

Chocolate Plus Que Parfait

Aline Ballentine ✤ Ellenville, NY

1 envelope unflavored gelatin mix
½ cup plus 1 tablespoon cold water
1 cup low-fat (2%) milk
¾ cup granulated sugar
3 eggs, separated
½ cup whipping cream
1 square (1 ounce) unsweetened chocolate, melted
¼ cup crème de menthe
1 to 2 drops green food coloring
Chocolate shavings
Mint leaves

1. Soften gelatin in 1 tablespoon water.

2. Combine remaining ½ cup water, milk, sugar and egg yolks in top of double boiler. Cook over boiling water, stirring constantly, until thick. Stir in gelatin; remove from heat. Cool until partially set.

3. Divide mixture into two medium bowls. Add whipping cream and chocolate to one bowl. Beat egg whites in small bowl with electric mixture until soft peaks form. Fold into plain gelatin mixture. Add crème de menthe and food coloring.

4. Alternate layers of chocolate mixture and mint mixture in 6 parfait glasses. Garnish with chocolate shavings and mint leaves.   *Makes 6 servings*

Gramma's Cannoli Cassata

Lois Gehrman ❧ Crescent City, CA

2 eggs
1½ quarts heavy cream
1 cup sugar
1 cup all-purpose flour
1 teaspoon grated lemon peel
½ cup ricotta cheese
½ cup finely chopped dried fruit
½ cup rum
¼ cup chopped pecans
2 teaspoons vanilla
1 homemade or store-bought pound cake (16 ounces), cut into ½-inch cubes

1. Whisk eggs and heavy cream in medium saucepan just until combined. Add sugar, flour and lemon peel, stirring to combine. Place saucepan over medium heat and cook, stirring constantly, until mixture begins to thicken, about 5 to 10 minutes. Remove from heat; stir in ricotta, pecans, dried fruit, rum and vanilla.

2. Place ⅓ of pound cake in tall trifle dish or deep serving bowl, distributing pieces to cover bottom of bowl. Top with ⅓ of cream mixture. Repeat layers 2 more times, ending with cream mixture. Cover with plastic cling wrap and refrigerate 4 hours or overnight. Serve cold. Garnish as desired.

Makes 12 servings

Lois Gehrman

Kentucky Bourbon Cake

Marie McConnell 🌿 Las Cruces, NM

4 cups all-purpose flour
2 teaspoons nutmeg
1½ teaspoons baking powder
3 cups chopped pecans
2 cups mixed candied fruit
2 cups raisins
2 cups orange marmalade
2 cups sugar
1½ cups butter or margarine, softened
6 eggs
½ cup molasses
¾ cup bourbon

1. Preheat oven to 300°F. Line two 10-inch tube pans with wax paper; grease well. Set aside.

2. Sift flour, nutmeg and baking powder into medium bowl; set aside. Combine pecans, candied fruit, raisins and marmalade in large bowl; add 1 cup flour mixture. Stir to coat well.

3. Beat sugar and butter in large bowl with electric mixer until fluffy. Beat in eggs, one at a time. Stir in molasses. Add half remaining flour mixture, then bourbon, beating well after each addition. Beat in remaining flour mixture. Stir in fruit mixture. Pour into prepared pans.

4. Bake 2 hours or until toothpick inserted near centers comes out clean. Cool 10 minutes. Remove from pans and cool completely. Wrap cakes in cheesecloth soaked with bourbon. Wrap in foil and let mellow for at least 2 days. *Makes 12 servings*

Marie says:

*After a day or so you can sprinkle on an extra ¼ cup bourbon
for more flavor.*

Roulage

Frances Golding 🌿 Northbrook, IL

5 eggs, separated
1 cup plus 1 tablespoon sugar
1 package (6 ounces) semi-sweet chocolate chips
3 tablespoon prepared coffee
4 tablespoons cocoa, divided
2 cups whipping cream
2 teaspoons vanilla

1. Preheat oven to 350°F. Grease jelly-roll pan and line with greased wax paper. Set aside.

2. Beat egg yolks in medium bowl with electric mixer until foamy. Gradually add 1 cup sugar.

3. Place chocolate chips and coffee in top of double boiler pan; stir until melted. Fold into egg yolk mixture.

4. Beat egg whites until stiff peaks form. Fold into chocolate mixture. Spread onto prepare pan. Bake 15 to 17 minutes.

5. Remove from oven. Place damp towel over cake for 30 minutes. Remove towel and sprinkle with 2 tablespoons cocoa. Invert cake onto wax paper. Peel off top piece of wax paper.

6. Beat whipping cream in medium bowl with electric mixer until stiff peaks form. Add remaining 1 tablespoon sugar and vanilla. Spread over cake to edges. Beginning at short end, roll cake jelly-roll style. Sprinkle with remaining 2 tablespoons cocoa. *Makes 10 servings*

Cheesecake-Filled Strawberries

Gina Cramer ⁊ North Branch, MI

1 package (8 ounces) cream cheese, softened
1½ tablespoons powdered sugar
1½ teaspoons vanilla
1 package (8 ounces) slivered almonds, toasted
1 pint strawberries

Beat cream cheese in medium bowl with electric mixture at medium speed 2 to 3 minutes. Add powdered sugar and vanilla; beat well. Trim bottom of strawberries. Scoop out inside of strawberries and fill with cream cheese mixture. Top each strawberry with 2 toasted almonds. Place strawberries on serving plate. Refrigerate until ready to serve.

Helpful Hint

To toast almonds, spread them on a baking sheet and place in a 350°F oven for 8 to 10 minutes, or in an ungreased skillet over medium heat until golden brown, stirring frequently. Always cool nuts to room temperature before combining them with other ingredients.

Chocolate Heaven on Earth

Zita Wilensky ❧ Miami, FL

1¼ cups graham cracker crumbs
¾ cup plus 3 tablespoons sugar, divided
3 tablespoons cocoa powder
¼ teaspoon cinnamon, divided
⅓ cup butter, melted
½ cup sliced toasted almonds, divided
1½ packages (8 ounces each) cream cheese, softened
2 eggs
1 tablespoon vanilla
1 tablespoon Tia Maria liqueur (optional)
1 container (8 ounces) sour cream
1 ounce semi-sweet chocolate, grated
1 ounce white chocolate, grated
Mocha Topping (recipe follows)
2 cups whipping cream

1. Preheat oven to 350°F.

2. Combine cracker crumbs, 3 tablespoons sugar, cocoa powder and ⅛ teaspoon cinnamon in medium bowl. Stir in butter. Press crumb mixture into 9-inch pie plate. Bake 8 minutes. Sprinkle with ¼ cup almonds.

3. Beat cream cheese and remaining ¾ cup sugar in large bowl with electric mixer until fluffy. Beat in eggs, vanilla, liqueur, if desired, and remaining ⅛ teaspoon cinnamon. Pour into prepared crust. Bake 30 minutes. Cool 15 minutes.

4. Spread sour cream on top of pie. Sprinkle with grated chocolate. Refrigerate.

5. Prepare Mocha Topping.

6. Pour Mocha Topping over pie. When ready to serve, beat whipping cream in medium bowl until stiff peaks form. Spoon over pie and sprinkle with remaining ¼ cup almonds. *Makes 8 to 10 servings*

Mocha Topping

1½ teaspoons instant coffee granules
2 tablespoons hot water
4 ounces semi-sweet chocolate
4 egg yolks
⅓ cup sugar
½ teaspoon vanilla

Dissolve coffee granules in water in medium saucepan over medium heat. Add chocolate and melt. Beat egg yolks in medium bowl with electric mixer. Gradually add sugar. Stir in chocolate mixture and vanilla.

Lemon Dessert

Billie Olofson ❦ Des Moines, IA

1 cup all-purpose flour
½ cup margarine, melted
½ cup chopped nuts
1 enveloped whipped topping, plus ingredients to prepare
1 cup powdered sugar
1 package (8 ounces) cream cheese, softened
2 packages (4-serving size each) lemon-flavored instant pudding mix
3 cups milk
Chopped nuts, for garnish

Preheat oven to 350°F. Combine flour, margarine and nuts in medium bowl. Press into 13×9-inch pan. Bake 15 minutes; cool completely. Set aside.

Prepare whipped topping according to package directions in medium bowl. Add powdered sugar and cream cheese; beat with electric mixer until well-combined. Spread over baked crust; set aside.

Combine pudding and milk in medium bowl. Spread over cream cheese layer. Spread whipped topping over pudding layer. Sprinkle with chopped nuts. Refrigerate until ready to serve. *Makes 10 to 12 servings.*

Chocolate Mint Eclair Dessert

Marie McConnell ❧ Las Cruces, NM

23 whole chocolate graham crackers
3 cups cold low-fat (2%) or fat-free (skim) milk
2 packages (4-serving size) white chocolate- or vanilla-flavored instant pudding mix
½ teaspoon mint or peppermint extract
3 to 4 drops green food coloring (optional)
1 container (8 ounces) frozen reduced-fat whipped topping, thawed
Cocoa Frosting (recipe follows)

1. Grease 13×9-inch baking dish with nonstick cooking spray. Line bottom of pan with three cracker halves and six whole crackers. Set aside.

2. Whisk milk and pudding mixes in large bowl 2 minutes. Whisk in extract and food coloring, if desired. Fold in whipped topping. Spread half of pudding mixture over graham crackers. Top with 3 graham cracker halves and 6 whole crackers. Spread remaining pudding mixture over crackers. Repeat graham cracker layer. Cover and refrigerate 2 hours.

3. Prepare Cocoa Frosting.

4. Spread Cocoa Frosting over graham crackers. Refrigerate until ready to serve.   *Makes 12 to 14 servings*

Cocoa Frosting

1 tablespoon butter
2 tablespoons cocoa
2 tablespoons plus 1 teaspoon low-fat (2%) or fat-free (skim) milk
1 cup powdered sugar
1 teaspoon vanilla

Melt butter in small saucepan. Stir in cocoa and milk until blended. Remove from heat; stir in powdered sugar and vanilla.

German Fruit Salad

Davon Burke 🌿 Emmet, AR

2 jars (16 ounces) maraschino cherries, drained
2 cans (11 ounces) mandarin oranges, drained
1 can (20 ounces) fruit cocktail, drained
1 container (16 ounces) sour cream
1 tablespoon mayonnaise
   Chopped walnuts (optional)
2 large red apples, cut into bite size pieces
2 bananas, cut into bite size pieces

1. Combine cherries, oranges and fruit cocktail in large bowl.

2. Combine sour cream and mayonnaise in medium bowl; stir into fruit mixture. Add chopped walnuts, if desired; mix well.

3. Cover; refrigerate 2 hours. Add apples and bananas just before serving; mix well. *Makes 8 servings*

Davon says:

This recipe may also be made with low-fat sour cream and mayonnaise.

Chocolate Mint Fluff Roll

Jane Shapton ❧ Tustin, CA

4 eggs, separated
¾ cup sugar, divided
½ cup butter, softened
¼ cup crème de menthe liqueur
2 tablespoons water
1 teaspoon vanilla
½ cup cocoa
⅔ cup cake flour
1 teaspoon baking powder
½ teaspoon salt
Chocolate Mint Filling (recipe follows)

1. Preheat oven to 375°F. Grease 15×10×1-inch jelly-roll pan. Line with greased parchment paper; dust with flour.

2. Beat egg whites in large bowl with electric mixer on high until soft peaks form. Gradually add ½ cup sugar, beating until egg whites are stiff and glossy. Set aside.

3. Combine egg yolks, remaining ¼ cup sugar, butter, crème de menthe, water and vanilla in small bowl. Beat until well combined. Fold thickened yolks into egg white mixture.

4. Sift cocoa, cake flour, baking powder and salt into medium bowl. Add dry ingredients to egg mixture and mix well, scraping sides and bottom of bowl.

5. Pour batter into prepared pan. Bake 12 to 15 minutes or until edges begin to pull away from sides of baking pan and center springs back when lightly touched. Dust a clean linen towel with powdered sugar. Invert cake onto towel. Peel off the parchment paper, and gently roll cake with towel, lengthwise. Cool cake completely. Prepare Chocolate Mint Filling.

6. Unroll cake, spread with filling, roll back up and place on serving plate. Sprinkle with more powdered sugar. Chill before serving.

Makes 8 to 10 servings

continued on page 172

Chocolate Mint Fluff Roll

Chocolate Mint Fluff Roll, continued

Chocolate Mint Filling

1½ **cups whipping cream**
½ **cup sugar**
¼ **cup cocoa**
¼ **cup crème de menthe liqueur**
½ **teaspoon vanilla**
   Dash salt
1½ **cups chopped chocolate mints**

Beat whipping cream, sugar, cocoa, crème de menthe, vanilla and salt in medium bowl. Continue beating until thick. Gently fold in mints.

Cherry Pie Blondies

Carol Jean Moeller ❧ *Fairview Park, OH*

1 **cup margarine**
1½ **cups sugar**
4 **eggs**
1 **tablespoon lemon juice**
2 **cups flour**
1 **can (21 ounces) cherry pie filling**
   Powdered sugar

1. Preheat oven to 350°F. Grease 15×10-inch jelly roll pan. Set aside.

2. Beat margarine in large bowl with electric mixer. Add sugar and beat until mixture is pale yellow and fluffy. Beat in eggs, one at a time. Add lemon juice. Add flour and beat until well blended.

3. Spread batter into prepared pan. Top with cherry pie filling, spreading to cover cake batter. Bake 30 minutes or until cake is light, golden brown. Cool in pan on wire rack. Sprinkle with powdered sugar just before serving.

Makes about 20 bars

Pineapple Meringue Torte
Catherine Reiter ❧ Altoona, WI

6 egg whites
2 cups plus 2 tablespoons granulated sugar, divided
1 teaspoon vanilla
1 teaspoon vinegar
1 pint whipping cream
1 can (20 ounces) crushed pineapple, well-drained
2 tablespoons powdered sugar
  Pecans (optional)

1. Preheat oven to 325°F. Grease bottoms of two 9-inch round cake pans. Line pans with greased waxed paper.

2. Beat whites in large bowl with electric mixer until foamy. Gradually add 2 cups sugar, vanilla and vinegar; beat until stiff peaks form. Divide evenly between pans and smooth into even layers. Bake 1 hour or until completely dry. Carefully remove from pans while warm; cool completely on wire racks. Remove waxed paper.

3. Beat whipping cream in medium bowl until stiff, gradually add pineapple and powdered sugar.

4. Place 1 meringue layer on serving plate. Spread evenly with ¼ of pineapple mixture. Top with second meringue layer. Spread top and sides of torte with pineapple mixture. Sprinkle with pecans, if desired. Refrigerate overnight.

Makes 12 servings

❧ Catherine says: ❧

I start draining the pineapple as my first step, even before I start making the meringue, in order to allow it to drain completely.

Kids' Goodies

Cookie Crumb "Sundae"

Carrie Vredenburg ❧ Olathe, KS

1 package (about 18 ounces) chocolate creme-filled
    sandwich cookies
4 cups milk, divided
1 package (4-serving size) cheesecake-flavored instant
    pudding mix
1 package (4-serving size) chocolate fudge-flavored instant
    pudding mix
1 container (8 ounces) frozen whipped topping, thawed
12 to 16 maraschino cherries, drained

Place cookies in large resealable plastic food storage bag and crush
with rolling pin. Place ¾ of crumbs in bottom of 13×9-inch
baking pan. Combine 2 cups milk and cheesecake-flavored
pudding mix in large bowl. Prepare according to package
directions. Pour pudding evenly over cookie crumbs. Repeat with
remaining 2 cups milk and chocolate fudge-flavored pudding mix.
Pour evenly over cheesecake pudding. Spread whipped topping
over pudding. Sprinkle remaining cookie crumbs over whipped
topping. Top with maraschino cherries. Chill 1 hour before
serving. *Makes 12 to 14 servings*

❧ Carrie says: ❧

*This dessert can also be made in individual disposable
clear plastic cups. Decorate each with colored sprinkles (see
photo). Kids love them like this. They are great for birthdays,
holidays and picnics.*

Easy Fruit Dessert

Cynthia Chamberlain ❧ Blythe, GA

1 homemade or store-bought angel food cake
1 package (4-serving size) vanilla-flavored instant pudding mix, plus
    ingredients to prepare
3 medium bananas
1 package (16 ounces) thawed frozen strawberries, cut in half
    lengthwise
1 container (8 ounces) frozen whipped topping, thawed
    Whole strawberries, for garnish (optional)

Cut angel food cake into cubes. Place cubes into 2-quart glass serving bowl, covering bottom and ¼ way up sides. Prepare pudding according to package directions. Pour over cake cubes. Slice bananas and layer over pudding. Layer strawberries over bananas. Spread whipped topping over strawberries. Garnish with whole strawberries, if desired.

Makes 12 servings

Nicy Icy Dessert

Elinor Jane Smith ❧ Ocala, FL

½ gallon vanilla frozen yogurt
¼ cup sugar-free maple syrup
1 can (11 ounces) mandarin oranges, drained
½ cup seedless grapes
½ cup toasted pecans, broken into pieces
    Marachino cherries, drained (optional)

Soften frozen yogurt until it resembles thick soup. Place in large serving bowl. Swirl in maple syrup. Fold in oranges, grapes and pecans. Freeze until firm. Scoop into individual serving dishes when ready to serve. Top each serving with cherry, if desired.

Makes 10 servings

Cream Cheese Cupcakes

Laura T. Dowling 🌿 Belleville, NJ

> 3 packages (8 ounces each) cream cheese, softened
> 5 eggs
> 1 cup sugar
> 2½ teaspoons vanilla, divided
> 1 pint sour cream
> ¼ cup sugar
> 1 cup fresh pitted cherries, fresh blueberries or crushed pineapple, drained

1. Preheat oven to 325°F. Line 24 regular-size (2½-inch) muffin cups with paper muffin cup liners.

2. Beat cream cheese, eggs, sugar and 1½ teaspoons vanilla in large bowl with electric mixer until well blended.

3. Pour batter into each muffin cup, ¾ full. Bake 20 minutes or until light golden brown. Remove from oven; cool 5 minutes.(Cupcakes will drop down slightly.)

4. Combine sour cream, sugar and remaining teaspoon vanilla in medium bowl. Fill depression in cupcakes with sour cream mixture. Bake 5 minutes more. Cool 10 minutes. Remove from pans and cool completely.

5. Top cupcakes with desired fruit topping.   *Makes 24 cupcakes*

Rocky Road Brownies

Jamie H. Mozingo ❧ La Pine, OR

1 package (20 ounces) dark or double chocolate brownie mix, plus
    ingredients to prepare
2 cups mini marshmallows
½ cup chopped walnuts
3 bars (8 ounces each) chocolate, chopped

Prepare brownie mix according to package directions. Fold in marshmallows
and walnuts. Pour batter into 13×9-inch baking pan. Bake as directed on
packages. Immediately top hot brownies with chocolate.

Makes 10 to 12 brownies

Seven-Layer Dessert

Sophia Hoff ❧ Tripp, SD

½ cup margarine, melted
1 teaspoon vanilla
1 cup graham cracker crumbs
1 cup butterscotch chips
1 cup chocolate chips
1 cup shredded coconut
1 cup nuts
1 can (14 ounces) sweetened condensed milk

Preheat oven to 350°F. Pour margarine into 13×9-inch baking dish. Add
vanilla. Sprinkle cracker crumbs over butter. Layer butterscotch chips over
crumbs, followed by chocolate chips, coconut and nuts. Pour milk over
mixture. Bake 25 minutes or until lightly browned. Cut into bars.

Makes 12 to 18 bars

Dixie Dream
Lois Dowling ❧ Tacoma, WA

1 cup semi-sweet chocolate chips, melted
1 cup peanut butter, divided
1 cup finely chopped dry roasted peanuts
1 cup white chocolate chips, melted
1 cup cream cheese, softened
3 cups whipped topping, divided

Grease 11-inch round plate or pizza pan. Combine melted semi-sweet chocolate, ¾ cup peanut butter and nuts in medium bowl. Spread onto prepared plate and chill until firm. Beat remaining ¼ cup peanut butter, white chocolate and cream cheese in medium bowl until fluffy. Fold in 2 cups whipped topping. Spread over chocolate crust. Decorate with remaining 1 cup whipped topping. Refrigerate until ready to serve.   *Makes 12 servings*

Pineapple Whip
Pat Murray ❧ Bangor, ME

1 package (10 ounces) large marshmallows
1 can (20 ounces) crushed pineapple, undrained
1 cup heavy whipping cream

Cut each marshmallow into 4 or 5 pieces. Combine marshmallow pieces and pineapple with juice in large bowl. Chill 4 hours or overnight. Beat whipping cream in medium bowl with electric mixer until stiff peaks form. Fold into pineapple mixture. Refrigerate until ready to serve.   *Makes 6 to 8 servings*

❧ Pat says: ❧

This is terrific served over chocolate cake or brownies.

Raspberry Bars

Elsie Brodjeski ❦ Mentone, Ca

1¼ cups all-purpose flour
¾ cup sugar, divided
½ cup butter or margarine, cut into ½-inch pieces
1 egg, beaten
2 egg whites
¾ cup chopped pecans
¾ cup raspberry jelly or jam

1. Preheat oven to 350°F. Grease 9-inch square baking pan; set aside.

2. Combine flour and ¼ cup sugar in medium bowl. Add butter and rub into flour with fingers until fine crumbs form. Add egg; mix until dough holds together. Pat into smooth ball. Firmly press dough evenly into bottom of prepared pan. Bake 20 to 25 minutes or until crust is pale golden in color.

3. Immediately spread jelly evenly over warm crust.

4. Beat egg whites in medium bowl with electric mixer at high speed. Fold in remaining ½ cup sugar and pecans. Evenly spread egg white mixture over jelly.

5. Return pan to oven and bake 25 minutes more or until top is brown. Cool in pan about 1 hour. Cut into bars.   *Makes about 16 bars*

Cookie Milk Shakes

Helen Fan ❦ Cupertino, CA

1 pint vanilla ice cream
4 chocolate sandwich cookies or chocolate-covered graham crackers

Scoop ice cream into blender fitted with metal blade. Crush cookies in resealable plastic food storage bag with rolling pin or food processor. Place cookies in blender. Process until well-combined. Pour into 2 glasses. Serve immediately.   *Makes 2 servings*

Easy Banana Sundae Cake
Brenda Sue Davidson ✺ Punta Gordon, FL

2 ripe bananas
2 eggs
1½ cups granulated sugar
1⅓ cups buttermilk
½ cup butter, melted
3 cups self-rising flour
2 teaspoons vanilla, divided
1 pint whipping cream
½ cup powdered sugar
1 can (21 ounces) strawberry pie filling
Chocolate syrup

1. Preheat oven to 350°F. Grease two 9-inch round cake pans with nonstick cooking spray. Set aside.

2. Beat bananas in large bowl with electric mixer at low speed. Add eggs and granulated sugar; beat well. Add buttermilk and butter. Beat in flour, one cup at a time. Add 1 teaspoon vanilla. Beat at medium speed 2 minutes. Spread evenly into prepared pans.

3. Bake 30 minutes or until center springs back when lightly touched. Cool in pans 10 minutes. Remove from pans and cool completely on wire racks.

4. Beat whipping cream in medium bowl with electric mixer on high speed until very thick. Add remaining 1 teaspoon vanilla and powdered sugar.

5. Place one cake layer on serving plate. Frost top of cake with whipping cream mixture. Top with half can pie filling. Top with remaining cake layer. Frost top and sides of cake with remaining whipping cream mixture. Draw a circle around edges of cake with chocolate syrup. Fill circle with remaining half can pie filling. Cover and refrigerate until ready to serve.

Makes 10 to 12 servings

✧ *Brenda says:* ✧

Draw a wide heart and fill with strawberry pie filling instead of circle and serve for Valentine's Day or Mother's Day.

Marshmallow Brownie Bars

June Hershberger ❧ Keithville, LA

1 package (about 21 ounces) brownie mix, plus ingredients to prepare
2½ cups miniature marshmallows
½ cup butter
4 tablespoons unsweetened cocoa powder
⅓ cup cola
1 teaspoon vanilla
4 cups powdered sugar
1 cup chopped nuts (almonds, peanuts, pecans or walnuts)

1. Prepare brownies according to package directions for 13×9-inch pan. Remove from oven and immediately top with single layer of marshmallows. Place under broiler until marshmallows begin to brown.

2. Combine butter, cocoa powder and cola in medium saucepan. Cook and stir over medium heat until mixture comes to a boil. Remove from heat; add vanilla and stir until smooth. Add powdered sugar and nuts and stir 1 to 2 minutes more or until well combined. Pour over marshmallows and spread to coat evenly. *Makes about 18 brownies*

❧ June says: ❧

I often make this in a disposable aluminum pan. Then when it's time to serve I cut down the sides of the pan and peel it away. All that's left is to cut the brownies and clean up is a snap.

Fruit Pizza

Michelle Gray Monmouth, ME

1 package (18 ounces) refrigerated sugar cookie dough
1 package (8 ounces) cream cheese, softened
1 jar (7 ounces) marshmallow creme
½ cup sugar
1 tablespoon cornstarch
½ cup orange juice
¼ cup water
2 tablespoon lemon juice
⅛ teaspoon salt
1 banana, peeled and sliced
½ cup sliced strawberries
½ cup blueberries
1 kiwi, peeled and sliced

1. Preheat oven to 350°F.

2. Press cookie dough on pizza pan. Bake 15 minutes or until lightly browned.

3. Combine cream cheese and marshmallow creme in medium bowl. Spread onto baked cookie. Refrigerate.

5. Combine sugar and cornstarch in medium saucepan. Add orange juice, water, lemon juice and salt. Mix well. Bring to a boil over medium heat. Boil 1 minute, remove from heat and cool.

6. Arrange fruit pieces on pizza as desired. Drizzle glaze over fruit. Refrigerate until ready to serve.   *Makes 10 servings*

BUSINESS REPLY MAIL

FIRST-CLASS MAIL   PERMIT NO. 24   MT. MORRIS, IL

POSTAGE WILL BE PAID BY ADDRESSEE

EASY HOME COOKING
PO BOX 520
MT MORRIS IL 61054-7451

NO POSTAGE
NECESSARY
IF MAILED
IN THE
UNITED STATES

Graham Cracker Pudding

Margaret L. Rose ❧ Mentor on the Lake, OH

3 packages (4-serving size each) vanilla-flavored pudding mix (not
  instant), plus ingredients to prepare
1 package (15 ounces) graham cracker crumbs
1½ cups light brown sugar, divided
3 large bananas, divided

Prepare pudding mixes according to package directions. Sprinkle ⅓ of cracker
crumbs on bottom of 13×9-inch baking pan. Sprinkle ½ cup brown sugar
over crumbs. Slice 1 banana over brown sugar. Spread half of pudding over
bananas. Repeat layers using ⅓ of cracker crumbs, ½ cup brown sugar,
1 banana and remaining pudding. Sprinkle remaining ⅓ of crackers over
pudding and remaining ½ cup brown sugar over crumbs. Slice and layer
remaining banana over brown sugar. Refrigerate until ready to serve.

Makes 12 to 14 servings

Deep Fried Doughnuts

Leah T. Lipson ❧ Brooklyn, NY

3 eggs, beaten
¾ cup sugar
1 cup plain yogurt
1 cup sour cream
3½ to 4 cups flour
1 teaspoon baking powder
Powdered sugar

Combine eggs and sugar in large bowl. Add yogurt and sour cream; mix well.
Add flour and baking powder. Heat deep fryer until oil is boiling. Carefully
drop tablespoons of dough into oil, turning once. Fry until each side is deep
golden brown. Remove to paper towels. Sprinkle with powdered sugar.

Makes about 12 doughnuts

Fruit Medley

Joan Lasys ❧ Payson, AZ

½ cup dried apples
½ cup dried blackberries
½ cup dried blueberries
½ cup dried cherries
½ cup dried pears
½ cup dried peaches
½ cup dried plums
½ cup dried strawberries
1 package (4-serving size) cherry-flavored gelatin
1 cup cranberry juice
3 to 4 cloves
1 cinnamon stick
1 medium orange, unpeeled, cut in ⅛-inch slices
1 lemon, unpeeled, cut in ⅛-inch slices
½ cup sugar or more to taste

1. Place dried fruit in strainer and rinse under cold running water, breaking up any clumps. Drain well. Place in large (4-quart or larger) pot.

2. Dissolve gelatin mix in cranberry juice; pour over fruit. Add enough cold water to cover fruit. Add cloves, cinnamon and sliced orange and lemon. Stir to combine all ingredients. Bring to a boil over medium-high heat. Cook until dried fruits have become plump and soft. Remove from heat and let cool slightly. Taste dried fruit and add sugar to taste while liquid is still warm.

3. Transfer fruit and cooking liquid to serving bowl and refrigerate until ready to serve. Top with whipped cream or whipped sour cream just before serving.

Makes 16 servings

❧ Joan says: ❧

You can also use any fresh, firm fruits such as raw apples or pears in this medley.

Strawberry Delight
Judy C. Gibson 🍓 *Pikeville, KY*

1 cup strawberry pie filling
1 can (8 ounces) crushed pineapple, drained
1 cup pecans
1 cup sweetened condensed milk
1 container (12 ounces) frozen whipped topping, thawed

Combine all ingredients in large bowl. Cover and refrigerate 3 to 4 hours.
Serve in individual serving dishes. *Makes 4 servings*

Orange Delight
Doris Christopher 🍓 *McAllen, TX*

2 packages (4-serving size) orange-flavored gelatin
2 cups hot water
2 cups cottage cheese
1 cup orange juice
1 cup pineapple juice
1 cup pecans
1 can (20 ounces) crushed pineapple, well-drained
6 tablespoons sugar
½ cup mayonnaise
1 pint whipping cream, whipped to stiff peaks

1. Dissolve gelatin in hot water in large serving bowl. Set aside.

2. Meanwhile, place cottage cheese in strainer and rinse under cold running
water; drain thoroughly.

3. When gelatin has cooled and thickened, stir in cottage cheese and all
remaining ingredients, except whipped cream. Stir to combine. Refrigerate
until cool but not set; fold in whipped cream. Refrigerate 1 hour or until ready
to serve. *Makes 8 to 10 servings*

Cocoa Bottom Banana Pecan Bars

Shelia Meinhardt ❧ Burns Flat, OK

1 cup sugar
½ cup butter, softened
1 egg
1 teaspoon vanilla
5 ripe bananas, mashed
1½ cups all-purpose flour
1 teaspoon baking powder
1 teaspoon baking soda
½ teaspoon salt
½ cup chopped pecans
¼ cup cocoa

1. Preheat oven to 350°F. Grease 13×9-inch pan. Set aside.

2. Beat sugar and butter in large bowl with electric mixer. Add egg and vanilla; beat until well combined. Beat in bananas. Combine flour, baking powder, baking soda and salt in medium bowl. Add to banana mixture; mix well. Add pecans; mix well.

3. Divide batter in half. Add cocoa to one half. Spread cocoa batter into prepared pan. Spread remaining batter over cocoa batter and swirl with knife.

4. Bake 30 to 35 minutes or until edges are lightly browned and toothpick inserted into center comes out clean.   *Makes 12 to 14 servings*

Taffy

Helen Fan ❧ Cupertino, CA

1 cup sugar
1 tablespoon cornstarch
¾ cup light corn syrup
⅔ cup water
2 tablespoons margarine or butter
1 teaspoon salt
2 teaspoons vanilla
¼ teaspoon food coloring, any color (optional)

Lightly grease 12-inch oval baking dish. Set aside. Combine sugar and cornstarch in 2-quart saucepan. Add corn syrup, water, margarine and salt. Attach candy thermometer to side of pan, making sure bulb is submerged in sugar mixture, but not touching bottom of pan. Bring to a boil, stirring constantly. Continue boiling, without stirring, about 10 minutes or until sugar mixture reaches hard-ball stage (265°F) (see hint). Remove from heat. Stir in vanilla and food coloring, if desired. Pour into prepared pan. When cool enough to handle, pull taffy with well-greased hands until light in color and no longer shiny. Pull into longer strips, ½-inch wide. Cut strips into 1½-inch pieces. Wrap pieces is wax paper or plastic wrap.

Makes about 1 pound taffy

Helpful Hint

To test for hard ball stage without a candy thermometer, drop a small amount of mixture into very cold water. It should form a hard ball and hold its shape, but be pliable.

Chewy Peanut Butter Brownies

Tracy Ademisaye ❧ Winnetka, CA

¾ cup butter, melted
¾ cup creamy peanut butter
1¾ cups sugar
2 teaspoons vanilla
4 eggs, lightly beaten
1¼ cups all-purpose flour
½ teaspoon baking powder
¼ teaspoon salt
¼ cup unsweetened cocoa powder

1. Preheat oven to 350°F. Grease 13×9-inch pan. Set aside.

2. Combine butter and peanut butter in large bowl and mix by hand until well-combined. Stir in sugar and vanilla. Beat in eggs. Add flour, baking powder and salt, stirring until just combined. Remove 1¾ cups batter to small bowl; stir cocoa into reserved batter.

3. Spread cocoa batter evenly in bottom of prepared pan. Top with remaining batter. Bake 30 minutes or until edge begins to pull away from sides of pan. Cool completely in pan; cut into bars to serve.

Makes about 3 dozen brownies

Moon Cake

Helen Syfie 🍓 Omaha, NE

1 cup water
½ cup margarine
1 cup all-purpose flour
4 eggs
2 packages (4-serving size) French vanilla-flavored pudding mix plus
    ingredients to prepare
1 package (8 ounces) cream cheese, softened (optional)
1 container (8 ounces) whipped topping
    Chocolate syrup

1. Preheat oven to 400°F. Grease jelly-roll pan; set aside.

2. Combine water and margarine in medium saucepan; bring to a boil over medium-high heat. Remove pan from heat and stir in flour. Beat in eggs, one at a time. Spread batter on prepared pan. Bake 25 minutes until bubbly. Let cake cool to room temperature.

3. Meanwhile, prepare pudding according to package directions adding cream cheese, if desired. Spread over cake. Spread whipped topping over pudding and drizzle with chocolate syrup. Refrigerate at least two hours before serving.

Makes about 12 servings

Pineapple Dessert

Maria E. Cervantes 🍓 Chicago, IL

1 container (8 ounces) whipped cream cheese
1 can (14 ounces) sweetened condensed milk
3 can (20 ounces each) pineapple chunks or fruit cocktail, drained

Beat cream cheese and condensed milk in large bowl with electric mixer. Add pineapple chunks; beat well. Cover and chill in refrigerator overnight.

Makes 6 to 8 servings

Peanut Butter Squares

Sandra Portman ❧ *Buffalo Grove, IL*

2½ cups powdered sugar
1¾ cup graham cracker crumbs
1 jar (8 ounces) creamy or chunky peanut butter
1 cup butter or margarine, melted
1 teaspoon vanilla
1 package (12 ounces) milk chocolate chips

Combine powdered sugar, cracker crumbs, peanut butter, butter and vanilla in large bowl. Spread into 13×9-inch baking pan. Refrigerate until firm.

Place chocolate chips in microwavable dish. Microwave according to package directions. Pour over peanut butter mixture.   *Makes 12 to 14 squares*

Nutty Cinnamon Muffins

Loreatha Jones ❧ *St. Louis, MO*

1 cup packed brown sugar
⅔ cup butter, melted
2 eggs, beaten
2 teaspoons vanilla
1 cup pecans, chopped
½ cup flour
2 teaspoons cinnamon

Preheat oven to 350°F. Grease and flour 24-cup miniature muffin tins. Set aside. Combine brown sugar and butter in large bowl. Add eggs and vanilla; mix well. Combine pecans, flour and cinnamon in medium bowl. Stir into egg mixture until moistened. Fill muffin cups ⅔ full with batter. Bake 20 minutes. Cool completely.   *Makes 24 muffins*

Cookie Pizza Cake

LeeAnn Camut ❧ Warrinton, PA

1 package (18 ounces) refrigerated chocolate chip cookie dough
1 package (16 to 18 ounces) chocolate cake mix, plus ingredients
    to prepare
1 cup vanilla frosting
½ cup peanut butter
1 to 2 tablespoons milk
1 container (16 ounces) chocolate frosting
    Chocolate peanut butter cups or other candy pieces (optional
    Peanut butter chips (optional)

1. Preheat oven to 350°F. Coat 12-inch round pizza pan with nonstick cooking spray. Press cookie dough evenly into pan. Bake 15 to 20 minutes or until edges are golden brown. Cool in pan on wire rack 20 minutes. Loosen edges of cookie with knife. Turn pan over to release cookie. Set aside.

2. Prepare cake mix according to package directions. Grease 12-inch round pizza pan. Fill pan ¼ to ½ full with batter. (Reserve remaining cake mix for another use or discard.) Bake 10 to 15 minutes or until toothpick inserted into center comes out clean. Cool 15 minutes on wire rack. Gently remove cake from pan; cool completely.

3. Combine vanilla frosting and peanut butter in small bowl. Gradually add milk, one tablespoon at a time, until spreadable consistency is reached.

4. Place cookie on serving plate. Spread peanut butter frosting on top of cookie. Place cake on top of frosted cookie. Trim cookie to match the size of cake, if necessary. Frost top and sides of cake with chocolate frosting. Decorate with peanut butter cups, if desired. Cut into slices.   *Makes 12 to 14 servings*

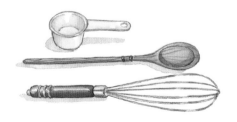

Perfect Peanut Butter Pudding

Lauren Silverman 🌿 Skokie, IL

2 cups milk
2 eggs
⅓ cup creamy peanut butter
¼ cup brown sugar
¼ teaspoon vanilla
¾ cup shaved chocolate or shredded coconut (optional)

1. Preheat oven to 350°F. Grease six (3-ounce) oven-safe custard cups; set aside.

2. Combine milk, eggs, peanut butter, brown sugar and vanilla in blender container; process on high 1 minute. Divide mixture evenly among prepared custard cups. Place cups in 13×9-inch pan; add enough hot water to come halfway up sides of custard cups.

3. Bake 50 minutes or until pudding is set. Remove from oven, then remove custard cups from pan and refrigerate until ready to serve.

4. Just before serving, top each cup with about ⅛ cup shaved chocolate or shredded coconut, if desired. *Makes 6 servings*

Cranberry Crunch Gelatin

Dorinda Ritter 🍓 Junction City, KS

1 package (3 ounces) cherry-flavored gelatin, plus ingredients to
    prepare
1 can (16 ounces) whole cranberry sauce
1 cup miniature marshmallows
1 cup coarsely chopped English walnuts

Prepare gelatin according to package directions. Chill until slightly set, about 2 hours.

Thoroughly fold in remaining ingredients. Chill until firm, about 2 to 3 hours.

Makes 6 servings

Simply Dreamy Cherry Cheesecake Squares

Kathleen Jamie Cannon 🍓 Meraux, LA

2 cups graham cracker crumbs
½ cup margarine, melted
1 package (4-serving size) cheesecake-flavored instant pudding mix
2 cups milk
4 cups frozen whipped topping, divided
1 can (21 ounces) cherry pie filling

Combine cracker crumbs and margarine in medium bowl and spread into bottom of 13×9-inch pan. Beat pudding mix and milk in medium bowl with electric mixer. Fold in 2 cups whipped topping. Pour over crumbs in pan. Spread pie filling over pudding mixture. Carefully spread remaining 2 cups whipped topping over pie filling. Refrigerate until chilled about 2 hours. Cut into squares.

Makes 12 to 14 servings

Brownie Pudding

Elaine Duesel ❧ Marlboro, MA

1 cup flour, sifted
⅔ cup sugar
6 teaspoons cocoa, divided
2 teaspoons baking powder
1 teaspoon salt
½ cup milk
2 teaspoons shortening, melted
1 teaspoon vanilla
1 cup brown sugar
1½ cups boiling water
    Vanilla ice cream (optional)

Preheat oven to 350°F. Grease 8×8-inch baking dish. Sift flour, sugar,
2 teaspoons cocoa, baking powder and salt into large bowl. Add milk,
shortening and vanilla; mix well. Pour into prepared pan. Combine brown
sugar and remaining 4 teaspoons cocoa in medium bowl. Sprinkle over batter.
Pour water over brown sugar mixture. Bake 30 to 40 minutes. Serve with ice
cream, if desired.   *Makes 8 servings*

Sticky Buns

Tami Crosby ❧ Glendale, AZ

24 frozen bread dough rolls, thawed
1 package (4-serving size) butterscotch-flavored pudding and pie
  filling mix (not instant)
½ cup firmly packed brown sugar
½ cup chopped pecans
½ cup butter or margarine, melted

Grease 12-cup Bundt pan. Layer rolls in pan. Sprinkle pudding mix, brown sugar and pecans over rolls. Drizzle butter on top. Cover pan with foil and refrigerate overnight.

Preheat oven to 400°F. Remove foil and bake 20 minutes or until lightly browned. Invert rolls onto serving plate. *Makes 24 servings*

❧ *Tami says:* ❧

Place a baking sheet underneath Bundt pan while baking to
catch drippings.

Holiday Traditions

Mom's Pumpkin Pie

Penny Nichols 🦋 *Baltimore, MD*

1½ cans (15½ ounces each) solid packed pumpkin
1 cup granulated sugar
1 can (12 ounces) evaporated milk
2 eggs
2 tablespoons maple syrup
1 teaspoon cinnamon
1 teaspoon vanilla
½ teaspoon salt
2 9-inch prepared pie shells
Whipped cream

Preheat oven to 350°F. Combine all ingredients, except pie shells and whipped cream, in large bowl; mix well. Divide mixture evenly between pie shells. Place pie pans on baking sheet. Bake 1 hour or until toothpick inserted into centers comes out clean. Cool completely. Top with whipped cream.

Makes 2 (9-inch) pies

Cranberry Dessert

Karen Schmidt ❧ Racine, WI

1½ cups sugar
½ cup butter
2 eggs
1 cup all-purpose flour
1 teaspoon baking powder
2 cups fresh or thawed frozen whole cranberries
¾ cup chopped nuts
Vanilla ice cream or whipped topping (optional)

1. Preheat oven to 350°F. Grease 10-inch pie pan. Set aside.

2. Beat sugar, butter and eggs in medium bowl with electric mixer. Add flour and baking powder. Stir in cranberries and nuts. (Dough will be stiff.) Spread into prepared pan.

3. Bake 45 minutes. Serve with ice cream or whipped cream, if desired.

Makes 10 to 12 servings

Tiger Butter-Peanut Butter Fudge

Alana Simpson ❧ Hokes Bluff, AL

1 package almond bark
2 tablespoons peanut butter
½ cup chocolate chips

Line baking sheet with waxed paper. Melt almond bark in medium saucepan. Stir in peanut butter. Pour peanut butter mixture over prepared baking sheet. Sprinkle with chocolate chips and swirl. Refrigerate until firm. Break into pieces.

Makes about 1 pound fudge

Holiday Delight

Ramona Wysong ❧ Barlow, KY

1 package (4-serving size) strawberry- or cranberry-flavored gelatin
¾ cup boiling water
¼ cup cold water
1 cup crushed ice
⅓ cup crushed pineapple, well-drained
⅓ cup chopped pecans
⅓ cup shredded coconut
⅓ cup miniature marshmallows

1. Combine gelatin and boiling water in small bowl. Stir until gelatin completely dissolves. Add cold water and ice; stir until mixture begins to thicken; remove any large pieces of unmelted ice.

2. Stir in remaining ingredients, being sure to coat marshmallows well.

3. Pour into decorative mold or serving bowl, tapping gently on counter to remove air bubbles. Refrigerate until completely set.   *Makes 6 to 8 servings*

❧ *Ramona says:* ❧

Top this delightful dish with whipped topping.

Spicy Raisin, Date & Candied Ginger Cobbler

Jim Lankford ✤ *Fredericksburg, VA*

⅔ cup granulated sugar
2 tablespoons cornstarch
2 cups seedless raisins
1 cup dates, pitted and chopped
1 cup orange juice
⅓ cup water
2 tablespoons candied ginger, finely chopped
3 tablespoons butter, divided
1 tablespoon lemon juice
½ teaspoon salt
1 small seedless orange, peeled, quartered and thinly sliced
1 can (10 ounces) flaky biscuits
2 tablespoons light brown sugar
Whipped cream (optional)

Preheat oven to 450°F. Combine granulated sugar and cornstarch in large saucepan. Stir in raisins, dates, orange juice, water and ginger. Bring to a simmer over medium heat, stirring constantly, until liquid is just thickened. Remove from heat. Stir in 1 tablespoon butter, lemon juice and salt. Fold in orange slices. Pour into 2-quart casserole dish. Separate biscuits in half. Cover top of raisin mixture with biscuit halves. Melt remaining 2 tablespoons butter. Brush butter onto biscuits. Sprinkle biscuits with brown sugar. Bake 10 minutes. *Reduce oven temperature to 350°F.* Bake 15 to 20 minutes or until biscuits are golden brown. Cool on wire rack until warm. Serve with whipped cream, if desired. *Makes 8 to 10 servings*

Spicy Raisin, Date & Candied Ginger Cobbler

Chocolate Yule Log with Mint Leaves

Helen Fan ❧ Cupertino, CA

11 eggs, separated
1 cup sugar
2 teaspoons vanilla, divided
⅔ all-purpose flour
2 tablespoons cornstarch
1½ cups milk
5 ounces bittersweet or semi-sweet chocolate, chopped
Chocolate-Rum Glaze (recipe follows)
Powdered sugar
12 to 15 mint leaves

1. Preheat oven to 350°F. Line jelly-roll pan with greased waxed paper. Set aside.

2. Beat 8 egg whites, ⅔ cup granulated sugar and 1 teaspoon vanilla in large bowl with electric mixer until fluffy and smooth. Add flour and whisk until smooth. Beat 8 egg yolks in separate large bowl with electric mixer until firm. Gently fold egg yolk mixture into egg white mixture. Pour batter onto prepared pan.

3. Bake 13 minutes or until puffy.

4. Beat remaining 3 egg yolks (reserve remaining egg whites for another use or discard), remaining ⅓ cup granulated sugar, cornstarch and remaining 1 teaspoon vanilla in large bowl with electric mixer. Set aside.

5. Bring milk to a boil over medium-high heat in medium saucepan. Pour 1 tablespoon milk into egg yolk mixture. Add egg yolk mixture to remaining milk. Bring to a boil, stirring constantly. Remove from heat. Add chocolate. Stir until chocolate is melted. Cover and refrigerate 2 hours.

6. Spread chocolate cream over cake. Roll cake, with waxed paper, jelly-roll style. Refrigerate overnight.

7. Prepare Chocolate-Rum Glaze.

8. Pour glaze over cake in thin layer. Sift powdered sugar over cake. Garnish with mint leaves.   *Makes 10 servings*

Chocolate-Rum Glaze

4 ounces semi-sweet chocolate, melted and cooled
½ cup heavy cream
1 tablespoon dark rum

Combine chocolate, cream and rum in large bowl. Beat with electric mixer until chocolate turns light in color.

Swedish Apple Pie

Billie Olofson 🌿 Des Moines, IA

4 apples, peeled, cored and sliced
1 cup plus 1 tablespoon sugar
1 tablespoon cinnamon
¾ cup butter, melted
1 cup all-purpose flour
1 egg
½ cup nuts (optional)

Preheat oven to 350°F. Fill 9-inch pie plate ¾ full with apple slices. Combine 1 tablespoon sugar and cinnamon in small bowl. Sprinkle over apples. Pour butter over apples. Combine remaining 1 cup sugar, flour and nuts, if desired, in medium bowl. Pour sugar mixture over apples. Bake 50 to 55 minutes or until top is golden brown.   *Makes 1 (9-inch) pie*

Lemon Gingerbread Trifle
Stephanie Overman ❧ Chatham, NJ

1 package (14½ ounces) gingerbread cake mix, prepared according to
  package directions
3 tablespoons sherry
¼ cup raspberry or strawberry preserves
2 cups raspberries or sliced strawberries
2 tablespoons toasted sliced almonds
1 package (4-serving size) lemon-flavored instant pudding mix,
  prepared according to package directions
1 container (8 ounces) frozen whipped topping, thawed

Cut gingerbread into 1-inch cubes. Layer half of the cake cubes in 2-quart
serving bowl. Sprinkle with half sherry. Layer ⅛ cup preserves, 1 cup
raspberries and 1 tablespoon almonds over cake cubes. Spread ½ pudding over
raspberries. Repeat layers using remaining cake cubes, sherry, preserves,
raspberries, almonds and pudding. Cover and chill 4 hours or overnight.
Spread whipped topping over pudding just before serving.

Makes 8 servings

Creme Drop Fudge
Alana Simpson ❧ Hokes Bluff, AL

1 package old-fashioned creme drops
1 cup peanut butter
½ cup pecans
½ cup shredded coconut (optional)

Melt creme drops in microwavable-safe bowl at HIGH 2 minutes. Immediately
add peanut butter, pecans and coconut, if desired. Pour into greased 8×8-inch
pan. Pat down with hand. Cool completely. Cut into squares.

Makes 12 to 16 servings

Pumpkin Bread

Fran Fitzgerald ❧ New City, NY

1 cup margarine
2 cups sugar
4 eggs, beaten
1½ cups canned pure pumpkin
3½ cups all-purpose flour
2 teaspoons baking soda
2 teaspoons cinnamon
1 teaspoons nutmeg
1 teaspoon salt
½ teaspoon ginger
½ teaspoon ground cloves
1½ cup semi-sweet chocolate chips
1 cup chopped walnuts
Cinnamon Nutmeg Glaze (recipe follows)

Preheat oven to 350°F. Grease two 9×2-inch loaf pans.

Beat margarine in large bowl with electric mixer until creamed. Add sugar; beat well. Beat in eggs and pumpkin; set aside

Combine flour, baking soda, cinnamon, nutmeg, salt, ginger and cloves in medium bowl. Gradually add to pumpkin mixture. Fold in chocolate chips and walnuts. Pour batter into prepared pans. Bake 60 to 70 minutes or until toothpick inserted into centers comes out clean. Cool.

Prepare Cinnamon Nutmeg Glaze. Pour glaze over cooled bread.
Makes 2 loaves (12 to 16 servings each)

Cinnamon Nutmeg Glaze: Combine 1 cup powdered sugar, ¼ teaspoon cinnamon and ¼ teaspoon nutmeg in medium bowl. Stir in 1 tablespoon milk.

Apple Crunch Pie

Jacki Remsberg ❧ Carson City, NV

1 refrigerated pie crust (½ of 15-ounce package)
1¼ cups all-purpose flour, divided
1 cup granulated sugar
6 tablespoons butter, divided
1½ teaspoons cinnamon, divided
¾ teaspoon nutmeg, divided
½ teaspoon ground ginger
¼ teaspoon salt
4 cups peeled, cored and diced apples
½ cup brown sugar
½ cup chopped walnuts

1. Preheat oven to 350°F. Place pie crust in pan and flute edge as desired.

2. Combine ¼ cup flour, granulated sugar, 2 tablespoons butter, 1 teaspoon cinnamon, ½ teaspoon nutmeg, ginger and salt. Stir to combine well. Add apples and stir to coat. Transfer to prepared pie crust.

3. Combine brown sugar and walnuts in small bowl. Sprinkle evenly on top of pie.

4. Bake 45 to 55 minutes or until filling is cooked through and solid.

Makes 8 servings

Little Christmas Puddings
Cindy Colby ❧ Park Ridge, IL

1 can (14 ounces) sweetened condensed milk
1 square (1 ounce) semi-sweet chocolate
2 teaspoons vanilla
2¼ cups chocolate sandwich cookie crumbs
⅓ cup white chocolate chips
Red and green decors

Combine sweetened condensed milk and semi-sweet chocolate chips in medium saucepan; cook over low heat until chocolate melts and mixture is blended, stirring constantly. Remove from heat; stir in vanilla.

Stir cookie crumbs into chocolate mixture. Cover with plastic wrap; refrigerate 1 hour.

Line baking sheet with waxed paper. Shape heaping teaspoonfuls crumb mixture into 1-inch balls. Place on prepared baking sheet. Refrigerate until firm.

Place balls in 1¾-inch paper or foil cups. Place white chocolate chips in microwavable bowl. Microwave at MEDIUM (50% power) about 2 minutes or until melted, stirring after each minute. Spoon melted white chocolate over tops of balls. Decorate with decors. Let stand until set. Store covered in refrigerator.

Makes about 3½ dozen treats

Pumpkin Bars

Jackie Remsberg ❧ Carson City, NV

4 eggs
1⅔ cups sugar
1 cup vegetable oil
1 can (15½ ounces) solid packed pumpkin
2 cups all-purpose flour
2 teaspoon cinnamon
2 teaspoons baking powder
1 teaspoon baking soda
1 teaspoon salt
Cream Cheese Icing (recipe follows)
1½ cups chopped pecans or walnuts, divided

1. Preheat oven to 350°F.

2. Beat eggs in large bowl. Gradually add sugar, oil and pumpkin, mixing well after each addition.

3. Sift flour, cinnamon, baking powder, baking soda and salt into medium bowl. Stir into pumpkin mixture. Fold in ½ cup pecans. Pour into ungreased 13×9-inch baking pan. Bake 25 to 30 minutes or until toothpick inserted into center comes out clean. Cool in pan on wire rack.

4. Prepare Cream Cheese Icing.

5. Top cake with Cream Cheese Icing, spreading evenly. Sprinkle with remaining 1 cup pecans. Cut into bars.   *Makes about 18 bars*

Cream Cheese Icing

2 packages (3 ounces each) cream cheese, softened
2 tablespoons butter or margarine
1 teaspoon vanilla
2 cups powdered sugar
1 to 2 tablespoons milk

Beat cream cheese in large bowl with electric mixer until fluffy. Add butter and vanilla; beat well. Add powdered sugar, ½ cup at a time, mixing well after each addition. Add milk until right spreading consistency is reached. Refrigerate until ready to use.

Scrumptious Truffles
Helen Fan ❧ Cupertino, CA

¾ cup heavy cream
10 ounces semi-sweet chocolate, chopped
2 tablespoons unsalted butter, cut into pieces
2 to 3 tablespoons brandy (optional)
½ cup unsweetened cocoa

Bring cream to a boil in medium saucepan over medium heat. Remove from heat and add chocolate; stir until melted. Add butter and brandy, if desired. Pour into large bowl. Chill 6 hours or overnight.

Form chocolate mixture into small balls with hands. Roll each ball in cocoa. Chill until ready to serve.   *Makes about 1 pound truffles*

Pistachio Nut Truffles: Prepare Scrumptious Truffles as above. Roll each truffle in finely chopped pistachios. Wrap in plastic wrap and chill up to 10 days.   *Makes about 1 pound truffles*

Chocolate Truffles: Prepare Scrumptious Truffles as above; freeze 1 hour. Melt 14 ounces semi-sweet, milk or white chocolate in medium saucepan. Dip each truffle in chocolate. Place on parchment lined baking sheet and chill in refrigerator until ready to serve.   *Makes about 1 pound truffles*

Raisin-Nut Cake

Jamie H. Mozingo ❧ La Pine, OR

1 cup granulated sugar
¾ cup packed brown sugar
½ cup shortening
1 cup buttermilk
3 eggs
2 cups plus 2 tablespoons all-purpose flour
1 teaspoon baking powder
1 teaspoon salt
¾ teaspoon baking soda
½ cup chopped walnuts
½ cup raisins

Preheat oven to 350°F. Grease two 9-inch loaf pans. Set aside. Beat sugars and shortening in large bowl with electric mixer at medium speed. Add buttermilk and eggs. Combine flour, baking powder, salt and baking soda in medium bowl. Gradually add flour mixture to sugar mixture. Fold in walnuts and raisins. Pour into prepared pans. Bake 1 hour or until toothpick inserted into centers comes out clean. Cool completely.

Makes 2 loaves (12 to 16 servings each)

Pecan Candy

Jessica Crum ❧ Rushsylvania, OH

2 cups sugar
½ cup water
2 teaspoons ground cinnamon
¼ teaspoon ground allspice
⅛ teaspoon ground nutmeg
1 teaspoon red food coloring
1 teaspoon vanilla
4 cups (16 ounces) pecans

Line baking sheet with foil and lightly grease; set aside. Combine sugar and water in medium saucepan; bring to a boil over medium-high heat, stirring constantly. Reduce heat to medium. Combine cinnamon, allspice and nutmeg in small bowl. Add spices and food coloring to sugar mixture; mix well. Continue stirring contstantly until mixture reaches 240°F (soft ball stage), about 5 minutes. Add vanilla and pecans. Immediately pour pecan mixture onto prepared pan; cool 5 minutes. Pull pecans apart in individual pieces. Cool completely. *Makes about 1 pound candy*

Jessica says:

This makes a great Christmas gift when put in a nice container.

A

Abuelita Arsenia's Favorite
    Dessert, 138
Airy Chocolate Cake, 154
Almonds
    California Gold Rush Rice
        Pudding, 98
    Cheesecake-Filled
        Strawberries, 164
    Chocolate Heaven on Earth,
        166
    Chocolate-Raspberry Layer
        Cake, 80
    Coconut Crunch Delight, 24
    Creamy Coconut Cake with
        Almond Filling, 86
    Mom's Heavenly Berry Cake,
        140
    Orange Bread, 117
Ambrosia, 98
Angel Food Cake Roll, 89
Angel Food Dream Cake, 129
Apple
    Apple Cake Dessert, 11
    Apple Crunch Pie, 210
    Apple-Pear Praline Pie, 38
    Apple Pita, 99
    Applesauce Cake, 19
    Apple Spice Cake, 92
    Baked Alaska Apple Butter
        Pie, 48
    Blueberry Yogurt Cake, 8
    Caramel Apple Bread
        Pudding with Cinnamon
        Cream, 100
    Caramel Apple Cheesecake,
        71
    Creamy Vanilla Apple Pie, 41
    French Vanilla Bread
        Pudding, 122
    Fruit Medley, 186
    German Fruit Salad, 169
    Mom's Apple Crisp, 96
    Mother's Sugarless Cake, 119
    Rustic Apple Tart with Crème
        Chantilly, 56
    Spicy Raisin Custard Pie, 42
    Swedish Apple Pie, 207
    Warm Apple & Blueberry
        Crisp, 116
    Zucchini and Apple Frosting,
        107
    Zucchini and Apple Pound
        Cake, 106
Apple Cake Dessert, 11
Apple Crunch Pie, 210
Apple-Pear Praline Pie, 38
Apple Pita, 99

Applesauce Cake, 19
Apple Spice Cake, 92
Apricot Fluff Shortcakes, 133
Aunt Lucille's Chocolate Pound
    Cake, 120

B

Baked Alaska Apple Butter Pie,
    48
Baked Custard, 104
Banana Cake, 6
Banana-Nut Cake with Brown
    Sugar Topping, 102
Banana Split Cake, 128
Banana Split Roll, 30
Banana Supreme Cake, 78
Blueberry
    Angel Food Dream Cake, 129
    Apricot Fluff Shortcakes,
        133
    Blueberry Crumb Cake, 111
    Blueberry Yogurt Cake, 8
    Easy Patriotic Layer Cake, 12
    Fruit Medley, 186
    Fruit Pizza, 184
    Glacéed Berries with Pink
        Meringue, 158
    Quick Berry Trifle, 142
    Warm Apple & Blueberry
        Crisp, 116
Blueberry Crumb Cake, 111
Blueberry Yogurt Cake, 8
Brandy Alexander Pie, 55
Brownie Pudding, 198
Brownies & Bars
    Cherry Pie Blondies, 172
    Chewy Peanut Butter
        Brownies, 191
    Cocoa Bottom Banana Pecan
        Bars, 188
    Date-Nut Orange Bars, 104
    Lemon Cheese Bars, 94
    Marshmallow Brownie Bars,
        183
    Peanut Butter Squares, 193
    Pumpkin Bars, 213
    Raspberry Bars, 180
    Rocky Road Brownies, 178
    Simply Dreamy Cherry
        Cheesecake Squares, 197
Brown Sugar Meringue, 49
Butter Brickle Cake, 93
Butter Custard Icing, 97
Buttermilk Pie, 60
Butterscotch Bundt Cake, 76
Butterscotch Cake, 6
Butterscotch Malt Zucchini
    Cake, 13

C

Cakes (*see pages 4-31 and*
    76-93)
    Airy Chocolate Cake, 154
    Angel Food Dream Cake, 129
    Aunt Lucille's Chocolate
        Pound Cake, 120
    Banana-Nut Cake with Brown
        Sugar Topping, 102
    Banana Split Cake, 128
    Blueberry Crumb Cake, 111
    Citrus Rum Cake, 148
    Cookie Pizza Cake, 194
    Easy Banana Sundae Cake,
        182
    Frozen Chocolate Cookie
        Cake, 144
    Kentucky Bourbon Cake, 162
    Lemon Chiffon Cake, 149
    Moist and Tender Carrot
        Cake, 108
    Mom's Heavenly Berry Cake,
        140
    Moon Cake, 192
    Mother's Sugarless Cake, 119
    Raisin-Nut Cake, 215
    Sunshine Cake, 97
    Zucchini and Apple Pound
        Cake, 106
California Gold Rush Rice
    Pudding, 98
Canadian Butter Tarts, 52
Caramel Apple Bread Pudding
    with Cinnamon Cream,
    100
Caramel Apple Cheesecake, 71
Caramel Snow Eggs, 155
Carrie's Carrot Cake, 16
Carrot Pineapple Cake, 83
Cheesecake Dessert, 139
Cheesecake-Filled Strawberries,
    164
Cherry Pie Blondies, 172
Chewy Peanut Butter Brownies,
    191
Chocolate
    Abuelita Arsenia's Favorite
        Dessert, 138
    Airy Chocolate Cake, 154
    Aunt Lucille's Chocolate
        Pound Cake, 120
    Brownie Pudding, 198
    Chocolate Frosting, 120
    Chocolate Ganache, 62
    Chocolate Heaven on Earth,
        166
    Chocolate Mint Eclair
        Dessert, 168

Chocolate *(continued)*
Chocolate Mint Filling, 172
Chocolate Mint Fluff Roll, 170
Chocolate Mousse, 155
Chocolate Plus Que Parfait, 159
Chocolate-Raspberry Layer Cake, 80
Chocolate Root Beer Rocky Road Pie, 53
Chocolate Rum Cake, 84
Cocoa Icing, 23
Cookie Crumb "Sundae," 174
Cookie Pizza Cake, 194
Cookies and Cream Layered Dessert, 132
Devil's Food Cake, 7
Double Dutch Choco-Latte Cheesecake, 75
Eclaire Dessert, 129
Five Layer Brownie Dessert, 90
Frozen Chocolate Cookie Cake, 144
Frozen Mocha Dessert, 136
Ganache-Topped Cheesecake, 62
Granny's No-Crust Chocolate Pie, 47
Jo's Moist and Delicious Chocolate Cake, 20
Julia Young's Chocolate Cake, 22
Little Christmas Puddings, 212
Neapolitan Cheesecake, 74
Nested Sweet Chocolate Mousse, 150
Peanut Butter Cup Cheesecake, 70
Rocky Road Brownies, 178
Scrumptious Truffles, 214
Triple Chocolate Pudding Cake, 28
Chocolate, Baking
Chocolate Cheesecake, 68
Chocolate Rum Glaze, 207
Chocolate Truffle Torte, 146
Chocolate Yule Log with Mint Leaves, 206
Italian Chocolate Pie alla Lucia, 46
Mocha Topping, 167
Scrumptious Truffles, 214
Chocolate Cheesecake, 68

Chocolate Chips
Banana Split Roll, 30
Chocolate Ganache, 62
Chocolate Mousse, 155
Chocolate-Peanut Butter Oatmeal Snacking Cake, 18
Chocolate Rum Cake, 84
Chocolate Truffle Torte, 146
Cookies 'n' Cream Cake, 14
Crunch Peanut Butter Chocolate Fudge, 135
Dixie Dream, 179
Fancy Fudge Pie, 36
Five Layer Brownie Dessert, 90
Neapolitan Cheesecake, 74
Peanut Butter Squares, 193
Pumpkin Bread, 209
Roulage, 163
Seven-Layer Dessert, 178
Tiger Butter-Peanut Butter Fudge, 202
Triple Chocolate Pudding Cake, 28
Chocolate Frosting, 120
Chocolate Ganache, 62
Chocolate Heaven on Earth, 166
Chocolate Mint Eclair Dessert, 168
Chocolate Mint Filling, 172
Chocolate Mint Fluff Roll, 170
Chocolate Mousse, 155
Chocolate-Peanut Butter Oatmeal Snacking Cake, 18
Chocolate Plus Que Parfait, 159
Chocolate-Raspberry Layer Cake, 80
Chocolate Root Beer Rocky Road Pie, 53
Chocolate Rum Cake, 84
Chocolate Rum Glaze, 207
Chocolate Truffle Torte, 146
Chocolate Yule Log with Mint Leaves, 206
Cinnamon Bake, 125
Cinnamon Nutmeg Glaze, 209
Citrus Cake, 31
Citrus Cream Cheese Frosting, 31
Citrus Custard Pie, 54
Citrus Rum Cake, 148
Cocoa Bottom Banana Pecan Bars, 188
Cocoa Frosting, 168
Cocoa Icing, 23
Coconut Cream Pie, 44
Coconut Crunch Delight, 24
Coffee Cake, 10

Cookie Crumb "Sundae," 174
Cookie Milk Shakes, 180
Cookie Pizza Cake, 194
Cookies 'n' Cream Cake, 14
Cookies and Cream Layered Dessert, 132
Créme Chantilly, 58
Cranberry Crunch Gelatin, 197
Cranberry Dessert, 202
Cream Cheese Cupcakes, 177
Cream Cheese Frosting, 17, 110
Cream Cheese Icing, 213
Creamy Coconut Cake with Almond Filling, 86
Creamy Vanilla Apple Pie, 41
Creme Drop Fudge, 208
Crumb Topping, 111
Crunch Peanut Butter Chocolate Fudge, 135

D
Daddy's Favorite Pineapple Pudding, 124
Date Loaf, 122
Date-Nut Orange Bars, 104
Deep Fried Doughnuts, 185
Delcious Strawberry Cake, 82
Devil's Food Cake, 7
Dixie Dream, 179
Double Dutch Choco-Latte Cheesecake, 75
Double Vanilla Cookie Parfait, 124

E
Easy Banana Sundae Cake, 182
Easy Fruit Dessert, 176
Easy Minty Lemon Pie, 40
Easy Patriotic Layer Cake, 12
Eclaire Dessert, 129
Egg Custard Pie, 50
Excellent Mint Wafers, 139

F
Fancy Fudge Pie, 36
Favorite Peanut Butter Pie, 32
Five Layer Brownie Dessert, 90
French Vanilla Bread Pudding, 122
Frostings, Glazes & Icings
Butter Custard Icing, 97
Chocolate Frosting, 120
Chocolate Rum Glaze, 207
Cinnamon Nutmeg Glaze, 209
Citrus Cream Cheese Frosting, 31
Cocoa Frosting, 168

Frostings, Glazes & Icings
(continued)
Cocoa Icing, 23
Cream Cheese Frosting, 17,
110
Cream Cheese Icing, 213
Icing, 83
Rum Butter Glaze, 85
Vanilla Cream Cheese Icing,
79
Zucchini and Apple Frosting,
107
Frozen Chocolate Cookie Cake,
144
Frozen Mocha Dessert, 136
Fruit Medley, 186
Fruit Pizza, 184

G
Ganache-Topped Cheesecake,
62
German Fruit Salad, 169
Ginger Spice Roll, 112
Ginger-Peachy Crisp, 110
Glacéed Berries with Pink
Meringue, 158
Golden Creme Cake, 17
Graham Cracker Pudding, 185
Gramma's Cannoli Cassata, 160
Grandma's Chamtorte Dessert,
103
Granny's No-Crust Chocolate
Pie, 47
Grilled Peaches with Raspberry
Sauce, 152

H
Hawaiian Delight Pie, 34
Hawaiian Fruit and Nut Quick
Bread, 114
Hawaiian Fruit Cake, 23
Hawaiian Paradise Pie, 59
Holiday Delight, 203

I
Icing, 83
Italian Chocolate Pie alla Lucia,
46

J
Jo's Moist and Delicious
Chocolate Cake, 20
Julia Young's Chocolate Cake,
22

K
Kathy's Key Lime Pie, 44
Kentucky Bourbon Cake, 162

L
Lazy-Daisy Cake, 4
Leftover Coffee Dessert, 118
Lemon Cheese Bars, 94
Lemon Chiffon, 134
Lemon Chiffon Cake, 149
Lemon Cream Cheese Pound
Cake, 25
Lemon Dessert, 167
Lemon Gingerbread Trifle, 208
Lemon Layered Dessert, 123
Lemon-Lime Pound Cake, 11
Lemon Meringue Pie, 61
Lemony Layers, 105
Little Christmas Puddings, 212
Low Carb Cream Cheese
Dessert, 69

M
Marshmallow Brownie Bars,
183
Marty Ann's Famous Southern
Pumpkin Cheesecake, 64
Mocha Topping, 167
Moist and Tender Carrot Cake,
108
Mom's Apple Crisp, 96
Mom's Bread Pudding, 113
Mom's Heavenly Berry Cake,
140
Mom's Pumpkin Pie, 200
Moon Cake, 192
Mother's Coconut Pie, 49
Mother's Sugarless Cake, 119

N
Nancy's Tiramisu, 156
Neapolitan Cheesecake, 74
Nested Sweet Chocolate
Mousse, 150
Nicy Icy Dessert, 176
Noodle Pudding, 107
Nuts (see also **Almonds**;
Pecans; **Walnuts**)
Banana-Nut Cake with Brown
Sugar Topping, 102
Caramel Apple Cheesecake,
71
Cranberry Dessert, 202
Dixie Dream, 179
Hawaiian Delight Pie, 34
Hawaiian Fruit and Nut
Quick Bread, 114
Hawaiian Paradise Pie, 59
Italian Chocolate Pie alla
Lucia, 46
Leftover Coffee Dessert, 118
Lemon Dessert, 167

Nuts (continued)
Marshmallow Brownie Bars,
183
Scrumptious Truffles, 214
Seven-Layer Dessert, 178
Nutty Cinnamon Muffins, 193

O
Orange
Ambrosia, 98
California Gold Rush Rice
Pudding, 98
Citrus Custard Pie, 54
Citrus Rum Cake, 148
Date-Nut Orange Bars, 104
Fruit Medley, 186
Fruit Pizza, 184
German Fruit Salad, 169
Kentucky Bourbon Cake, 162
Mother's Sugarless Cake, 119
Nicy Icy Dessert, 176
Orange Bread, 117
Orange Delight, 187
Orange Kiss Me Cake, 26
Spicy Raisin, Date & Candied
Ginger Cobbler, 204
Orange Bread, 117
Orange Delight, 187
Orange Kiss Me Cake, 26

P
Pam's Peanut Butter Balls, 144
Peanut Butter
Chewy Peanut Butter
Brownies, 191
Cookie Pizza Cake, 194
Creme Drop Fudge, 208
Crunch Peanut Butter
Chocolate Fudge, 135
Dixie Dream, 179
Favorite Peanut Butter Pie, 32
Pam's Peanut Butter Balls, 144
Peanut Butter Cup
Cheesecake, 70
Peanut Butter Fudge, 130
Peanut Butter Pie, 43
Peanut Butter Squares, 193
Perfect Peanut Butter
Pudding, 196
Tiger Butter-Peanut Butter
Fudge, 202
Pecans
Airy Chocolate Cake, 154
Apple-Pear Praline Pie, 38
Banana Split Cake, 128
Butterscotch Bundt Cake, 76
Chocolate Root Beer Rocky
Road Pie, 53

Pecans *(continued)*
  Chocolate Rum Cake, 84
  Citrus Rum Cake, 148
  Cocoa Bottom Banana Pecan
    Bars, 188
  Cocoa Icing, 23
  Coffee Cake, 10
  Creme Drop Fudge, 208
  Date-Nut Orange Bars, 104
  Fancy Fudge Pie, 36
  Gramma's Cannoli Cassata,
    160
  Hawaiian Fruit Cake, 23
  Hawaiian Paradise Pie, 59
  Kentucky Bourbon Cake,
    162
  Moist and Tender Carrot
    Cake, 108
  Nested Sweet Chocolate
    Mousse, 150
  Nicy Icy Dessert, 176
  Nutty Cinnamon Muffins,
    193
  Orange Delight, 187
  Pecan Candy, 216
  Raspberry Bars, 180
  Sticky Buns, 199
  Strawberry Delight, 187
  White Chocolate Pecan
    Caramel Cheesecake, 72
  Yum-Yum Cake, 29
Penelope's Favorite Pumpkin
  Pie, 37
Perfect Peanut Butter Pudding,
  196
Pies *(see pages 32-61)*
  Apple Crunch Pie, 210
  Mom's Pumpkin Pie, 200
  Swedish Apple Pie, 207
Pineapple Cheesecake, 65
Pineapple-Coconut Cake, 88
Pineapple Coconut Poundcake,
  79
Pineapple Cream Cheese Pie, 35
Pineapple Delight, 92
Pineapple Dessert, 192
Pineapple Meringue Torte,
  173
Pineapple Whip, 179
Pumpkin Bars, 213
Pumpkin Bread, 209
Pumpkin Spice Cake, 88

Q
Quick Berry Trifle, 142

R
Raisin-Nut Cake, 215

Raspberry
  Chocolate-Raspberry Layer
    Cake, 80
  Easy Patriotic Layer Cake, 12
  Grilled Peaches with
    Raspberry Sauce, 152
  Lemon Gingerbread Trifle,
    208
  Quick Berry Trifle, 142
  Raspberry Bars, 180
  Raspberry Cream Pie, 50
Raspberry Bars, 180
Raspberry Cream Pie, 50
Red Velvet Cake, 85
Rhubarb Tart, 117
Rocky Road Brownies, 178
Root Beer Float Cheesecake, 66
Roulage, 163
Rum Butter Glaze, 85
Rustic Apple Tart with Crème
  Chantilly, 56
Rustic Tart Crust, 58

S
Scrumptious Truffles, 214
Seven-Layer Dessert, 178
Simply Dreamy Cherry
  Cheesecake Squares, 197
Speedy Strawberry Pie, 52
Spiced Filling, 113
Spiced Raisin Custard Pie, 42
Spicy Crumb Topping, 41
Spicy Raisin, Date & Candied
  Ginger Cobbler, 204
Sticky Buns, 199
Strawberry
  Cheesecake-Filled
    Strawberries, 164
  Delcious Strawberry Cake, 82
  Easy Banana Sundae Cake,
    182
  Easy Fruit Dessert, 176
  Fruit Medley, 186
  Fruit Pizza, 184
  Glacéed Berries with Pink
    Meringue, 158
  Mom's Heavenly Berry Cake,
    140
  Quick Berry Trifle, 142
  Speedy Strawberry Pie, 52
  Strawberry Angel Food
    Dessert, 134
  Strawberry Delight, 187
  Strawberry Delight Salad, 133
  Strawberry Dessert, 145
  Strawberry Salad, 135
Strawberry Angel Food Dessert,
  134

Strawberry Delight, 187
Strawberry Delight Salad, 133
Strawberry Dessert, 145
Strawberry Salad, 135
Sunshine Cake, 97
Swedish Apple Pie, 207

T
Taffy, 190
Tammy's Triple Banana Treat,
  141
Tiger Butter-Peanut Butter
  Fudge, 202
Triple Chocolate Pudding Cake,
  28

V
Vanilla Cream Cheese Icing, 79
Vanilla Ice Cream Loaf, 126
Vinegar Stew, 105

W
Walnuts
  Apple Crunch Pie, 210
  Applesauce Cake, 19
  Banana Supreme Cake, 78
  Blueberry Yogurt Cake, 8
  Butter Brickle Cake, 93
  Canadian Butter Tarts, 52
  Carrie's Carrot Cake, 16
  Cinnamon Nutmeg Glaze,
    209
  Cranberry Gelatin, 197
  Crumb Topping, 111
  Orange Kiss Me Cake, 26
  Pumpkin Bread, 209
  Raisin-Nut Cake, 215
  Rocky Road Brownies, 178
  Strawberry Delight Salad, 133
  Tammy's Triple Banana Treat,
    141
  Warm Apple & Blueberry Crisp,
    116
  White Chocolate Pecan Caramel
    Cheesecake, 72

Y
Yum-Yum Cake, 29

Z
Zucchini and Apple Frosting,
  107
Zucchini and Apple Pound
  Cake, 106

METRIC CONVERSION CHART

VOLUME MEASUREMENTS (dry)

$1/8$ teaspoon = 0.5 mL
$1/4$ teaspoon = 1 mL
$1/2$ teaspoon = 2 mL
$3/4$ teaspoon = 4 mL
1 teaspoon = 5 mL
1 tablespoon = 15 mL
2 tablespoons = 30 mL
$1/4$ cup = 60 mL
$1/3$ cup = 75 mL
$1/2$ cup = 125 mL
$2/3$ cup = 150 mL
$3/4$ cup = 175 mL
1 cup = 250 mL
2 cups = 1 pint = 500 mL
3 cups = 750 mL
4 cups = 1 quart = 1 L

VOLUME MEASUREMENTS (fluid)

1 fluid ounce (2 tablespoons) = 30 mL
4 fluid ounces ($1/2$ cup) = 125 mL
8 fluid ounces (1 cup) = 250 mL
12 fluid ounces ($1 1/2$ cups) = 375 mL
16 fluid ounces (2 cups) = 500 mL

WEIGHTS (mass)

$1/2$ ounce = 15 g
1 ounce = 30 g
3 ounces = 90 g
4 ounces = 120 g
8 ounces = 225 g
10 ounces = 285 g
12 ounces = 360 g
16 ounces = 1 pound = 450 g

DIMENSIONS

$1/16$ inch = 2 mm
$1/8$ inch = 3 mm
$1/4$ inch = 6 mm
$1/2$ inch = 1.5 cm
$3/4$ inch = 2 cm
1 inch = 2.5 cm

OVEN TEMPERATURES

250°F = 120°C
275°F = 140°C
300°F = 150°C
325°F = 160°C
350°F = 180°C
375°F = 190°C
400°F = 200°C
425°F = 220°C
450°F = 230°C

BAKING PAN SIZES

Utensil	Size in Inches/Quarts	Metric Volume	Size in Centimeters
Baking or	8×8×2	2 L	20×20×5
Cake Pan	9×9×2	2.5 L	23×23×5
(square or	12×8×2	3 L	30×20×5
rectangular)	13×9×2	3.5 L	33×23×5
Loaf Pan	8×4×3	1.5 L	20×10×7
	9×5×3	2 L	23×13×7
Round Layer	8×1½	1.2 L	20×4
Cake Pan	9×1½	1.5 L	23×4
Pie Plate	8×1¼	750 mL	20×3
	9×1¼	1 L	23×3
Baking Dish	1 quart	1 L	—
or Casserole	1½ quart	1.5 L	—
	2 quart	2 L	—

Do you have your own favorite original recipe? We'd love to hear about it! Send it in, along with the submission form below. Your recipe could be chosen for one of our upcoming cookbooks!

:: HOME-TESTED :: RECIPES pil

SUBMISSION FORM

Please attach to your recipe

Name:_____

Address:_____

City:_____ State:_____ Zip:_____

Phone:_____ Email:_____

Recipe Name:_____

Category (Check One): ❏ **Slow Cooker** ❏ **Desserts**
                               ❏ **Casseroles** ❏ **Cookies**

Mail to: Home-Tested Recipes, Cookbook Dept., Publications International, Ltd., 7373 N. Cicero Ave., Lincolnwood, IL 60712

Do you have your own favorite original recipe? We'd love to hear about it! Send it in, along with the submission form below. Your recipe could be chosen for one of our upcoming cookbooks!

HOME-TESTED
RECIPES
pil

SUBMISSION FORM
Please attach to your recipe

Name:_____

Address:_____

City:_____ **State:**_____ **Zip:**_____

Phone:_____ **Email:**_____

Recipe Name:_____

Category (Check One): ❑ **Slow Cooker** ❑ **Desserts**
                        ❑ **Casseroles** ❑ **Cookies**

Mail to: Home-Tested Recipes, Cookbook Dept., Publications International, Ltd., 7373 N. Cicero Ave., Lincolnwood, IL 60712